PANDEMIC
CASH FLOW

Cash Flow management
changes businesses and lives.
Thanks for taking on
the problem!

I hope you enjoy my book.

Bein

PANDEMIC
CASH FLOW

Cash flow issues kill nearly 30%
of businesses. Why it happens,
and how to prevent it.

Blaine Bertsch

Edited by Barbara Easter

First Edition

"We were always focused on our profit and loss statement. But cash flow was not a regularly discussed topic. It was as if we were driving along, watching only the speedometer, when in fact we were running out of gas."

—Michael Dell, founder and CEO, Dell Technologies

Who Should Read This Book

Business owners. When it comes down to it - your ass is on the line and you have the most to lose.

Business support, bookkeepers, accountants, fractional CFOs, and business coaches need to know how to deconstruct concepts around cash flow, how to talk about it with each other and with clients, and how to bring action to success.

Banks and investors. You have money in the mix and without a working understanding of cash flow, you continue to be at risk for failures that cost you money, personnel, and knowledge.

Contents

Appendix 213

Acknowledgments

I decided to take up the war on cash flow problems around 2012. This book is just one of the many battles along the way and it's been a long but rewarding journey. First and foremost, I'd like to thank my wife, Heather, for her unending support, patience and insight right from day one.

This book is the culmination of a couple of decades in the trenches of small business. The experiences, problems, and sleepless nights are shared with business owners across the globe. Through hundreds of candid and honest conversations, a workable solution started to take form. There have been so many friends, family, colleagues, mentors and advisors along the way that have helped immensely. I wish I could name every one of you but it would fill up the book!

If we've talked, I thank you with all of my heart. Every conversation has helped with my understanding, fed me with energy and helped me carry on through the tough times.

Foreword

There is no correlation between profit & promises.

You must believe that managing your cash flow will give you a pulse on your business.

As you read *Pandemic Cash Flow*, remember that your budget is the roadmap, the balance sheet provides insights into how well you are doing, while cash flow forecast is the day-to-day itinerary for your organization. Without an itinerary or cash flow forecast, you are in dire trouble.

Inspired by Blaine Bertsch the founder of Dryrun.com, *Pandemic Cash Flow* will provide you with practical tools, which will ensure that your business is disciplined, accountable and optimizing its resources.

From business owners through to bookkeepers, accountants and financial CFO's, *Pandemic Cash Flow* will:

- Give you a handle on the concrete facts that provide the fuel to grow and expand your business.

- Provide an understanding of the appropriate metrics to measure, Cash is King!

- Highlight specific solutions, processes and systems to implement.

- Help you set revenue goals, forecast and manage profits.

Within the appendix, be sure to take the Cash Flow Check Up. It is here, where we will guide you through the simple process to build a Scorecard to manage a handful of metrics so you can recognize your current limitations.

Let's work with discipline & accountability; report on a handful of metrics and gain traction.

It's in your best interest to invest in a world-class cash flow tool that serves as a universal translator between you and your accountant. You should absolutely check out dryrun.com

Remember, there's gold in the numbers.

Scott Rusnak
Certified EOS / Traction Implementer

www.ScottRusnak.com

Preface

Here I was…staring at a blank spreadsheet. No clue where to start. But I knew if I didn't get started, my business would fail.

It was 2009 and the global recession was working its way into our business. It wasn't just on the news anymore. Client budgets were slamming shut on all sides, projects were canceled mid-stream, and to make it worse, we'd just expanded our team, moved to a bigger office and leased fancy new sports cars.

Brilliant move.

I'll be honest with you. I'm not sure I even knew the term 'cash flow'. But I knew the concept. I'd made the lonely walk to the mailbox pleading that a check had rolled in to save us. Meanwhile, we'd dumped personal funds into the business accounts to keep us afloat.

How did we get here? How did I not see this coming?

What a mess.

I started my first business in 1999. At that point, it was just me. Somehow, over the years things just kept getting a little bigger. Projects got bigger, the team grew larger, and expenses grew at a feverish pitch. Somehow, it didn't feel like the profit matched the growing risk but I really didn't pay that much attention.

The years leading up to 2009 were a different story. It always felt like new business and repeat clients were walking in the door. We were constantly on 'trade trips' and going to conferences. We were trying to uncover the 'next big thing' for our business. Honestly, it just feels bizarre to me today. New

York, Austin, Hong Kong, Shanghai... Fun but not necessarily profitable.

So, back to 2009: I'm sitting in my oversized office, staring at a spreadsheet. What did I know about spreadsheets? A thousand little boxes filled my screen and somehow this was going to help me figure things out.

Now what? Well, top of my mind, can we make payroll on Friday? I guess I'll just work backward from that point and figure it out. I gathered up contracts, invoices, bills, payroll statements... whatever I could gather. Pretty much everything was still paper in those days, sitting in binders and folders scattered throughout the office.

How much DID it cost to stay in business every month? Budget time. I think I had a decent tally but I needed something with some structure. I needed more detail and data that looked forward into the coming weeks and months. It was too late to change yesterday. We were down to nickels and dimes so a 'rough guess' wasn't going to cut it.

A little digging while learning the ins and outs of spreadsheet usage and I had built a budget. I knew where our break-even point was, at least with the regular monthly costs.

Now I needed to figure out what bills were sitting on my desk along with the ones that would roll in over the next little while that weren't "the usual." The tax bill, invoices from contractors and suppliers, the hard drive desperately needed for the editing suite. I added them all to the list. This was going to get messy.

But once I had a handle on the next month or two's expenses, I could finally figure out if we would have enough income to cover everything. I dug out our invoices and went to work.

First of all, I just listed the invoices and grabbed a total. Well, that was a waste of time. If I didn't know when the money would show up in our mailbox, get deposited into the account…then wait on the bank to grant us access to our funds, I'd be out of luck.

That's when reality hit me. The numbers were only half the story. The other, even more important part, was the timing. Would the invoice be paid, cash in the bank, before the bills and expenses needed to be dealt with?

I need another spreadsheet. (Well that was something I didn't think I'd ever say.)

This one was all about the timing of the payments. I guess I could have just tried to add more and more data to the first sheet but it was already massive. I needed to simplify things. Stand back, look at where we were at and make some decisions. I needed it to be simple and clear.

Over the weeks and months, I went from dreading the process to getting addicted to data. Soon, I had spreadsheets all over the place. Not only did I build a system for tracking our cash flow, I even built a sales projection that had all of our potential deals and when I thought they could turn into money. I explored our profit margins and staff efficiency. I began to uncover the truth behind our business.

Finally, I was working on my business rather than in my business. By this point, we were closing in on 2011 when I made a realization. We were leaving a ton of cash on the table that should be powering our growth. And we'd left even more on the table in the first few years of business with our 'fly-by-the-seat-of-our-pants' methodology.

There truly was gold in the numbers.

Part 1

Understanding the Problem

Cash is King

So why is cash flow a 'pandemic?' Sounds like an exaggeration, right? Here are some stats:

Half of all businesses will fail within their first five years and cash flow issues are the leading cause.[1] In fact nearly 30% of businesses will fail due to cash flow issues alone[2] and 82% of every business that fails places blame on cash flow.[3]

According to Finpacific, 70% of businesses that fail are profitable when they close their doors. Further, they note that businesses only planning once a year have a 36% survival rate over five-years versus those planning monthly, which have an 80% survival rate.

Globally, one out of four businesses will die from cash flow issues. In any other domain, that would be considered a pandemic. Somehow, in business, this frightening statistic is seen as just part of the game. It doesn't have to be that way.

Cash flow forecasting and management can help turn the tide and save businesses, personal fortunes, savings and sleepless nights.

As terrifying as these stats may be, the greatest tragedy is that those aren't just numbers. The numbers represent people. Business owners with their life savings on the line, families they support, staff that need their paychecks to keep their households running. In the end, the cash flow pandemic is a crushing blow to people who are trying to make a difference in the world.

So what is cash flow?

Formally, cash flow refers to the money that is received by the business as well as what the business pays out. Even though it's referred to as 'cash', the truth is that, in today's businesses, very little of those funds called cash flow might be in the form of actual cash.

Inflows of money may come in via deposits from credit card purchases, electronic payments or even paper checks. The defining factor is that the payments coming in aren't 'cash flow' until you have access to the funds from your bank account or even your cash register.

Conversely, outflows of money aren't considered part of the cash flow until they leave your bank account or your pocket.

Cash flow is a simple concept, but with all of the various ways to get paid and make payments, coupled with the delays tied to future due dates, late and even default payments, tracking cash flow becomes extremely complicated.

It's a real puzzle to decode when money is likely to come and go from your accounts, compounded when an outgoing payment occurs before money arrives to cover the expense.

As complicated as this near-term cash flow is for businesses to manage, poor timing and late payments are not the only factors involved in cash flow shortfalls.

Often, a cash flow problem can be related to larger, systemic issues that will kill a business if they're not uncovered and addressed. Revenue shortfalls lead the way. Simply put, if your business needs to make $1 million this year to break even, you need the cash coming in over twelve months, not fourteen.

There's one other thing that keeps your business afloat when things are going well, but can also doom a business when it falls short, and that's profit. If it costs you $1.2 million to generate $1 million of revenue, your business is in trouble. You need to make $1 million in revenue while spending less than $1 million. Whatever is left over is your profit. A business with plenty of revenue but negative profit margins will slowly bleed to death.

In this book, we will focus on the short-term cash flow issues that tragically kill businesses nearly overnight but we'll also discuss the overarching issues as well to ensure that you're paying attention to all three legs of your business, your revenue, profit and cash flow.

Revenue, Profit & Cash Flow Crash Course

Let's take a bit of a closer, more formal view of these three factors:

Revenue

Revenue refers to the income your business has earned from the sale of your goods and services. Your revenue may also include money earned from other sources, such as interest, fees and royalties. Revenue is generally described in terms of a specific time period, such as revenue in a particular month, quarter, or year.

For instance, if a service company invoiced $100,000 in March, then they have earned revenue of $100,000 for that month. In this case, the business is not receiving payment in actual cash; rather it is 'owed' $100,000. In accounting terms, once they've invoiced a customer the amount is considered revenue (and you have to pay tax on that money, whether you've received it or not - how's that for a real kick in the backside!)

A business may have revenue in a particular time period that includes invoices that have been sent out to customers, as well as cash payments from customers at the time of purchase. All of these sales are included as revenue during that time period.

If you were referring to your Income Statement from the month of March, the top line of that statement would contain the $100,000 in revenue.

The term 'revenue' is commonly used in other situations in business. For instance, you may say that you've earned more revenue from the sales of a specific product compared to

Fig 1. Revenue, Profit and Cash Flow

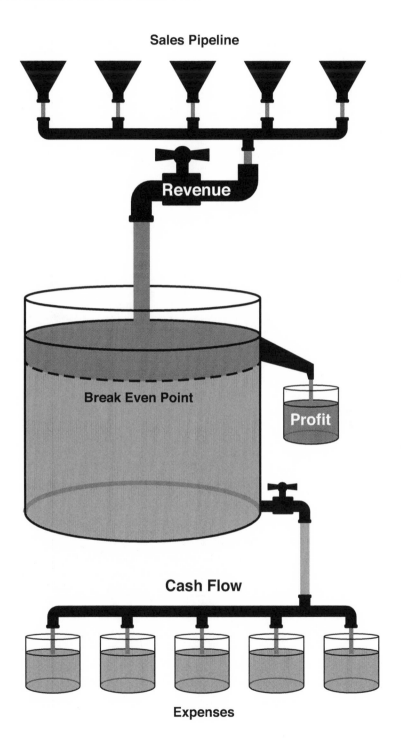

another. You may also ask what revenue was earned for a particular contract or from a specific customer.

In these cases, revenue refers to the income or earnings in each situation but may not refer to a particular period. 'Revenue' never accounts for expenses and costs. It simply describes total money earned by the business.

So, if you had a single contract to perform a service for a customer and the contract was worth $50,000, then your revenue for the project was $50,000.

If you got to the end of the year and looked at all of your sales, both cash and invoiced amounts, you could tally that up to see your revenue for that year.

But that doesn't mean those invoices have been paid yet…

Profit

In the simplest terms, profit is the result of your revenue minus your expenses.

So, earning a profit means that you've made more money than it costs to deliver the goods or services. In our revenue example above, the single contract was worth $50,000. If it cost your business $40,000 to provide that service, the resulting profit on the contract would be $10,000.

Going a little more in-depth, there are two types of profit. Gross profit and net profit. These two figures are used in determining your gross profit margin and your net profit margin.

Gross Profit

Your 'gross profit' calculates the revenue from your goods or services minus the cost of goods sold or 'COGS.' It's important to note that your gross profit only accounts for expenses directly related to the creation of those specific goods and services. Not other expenses.

Example: if you manufacture wooden boxes, the direct costs may include the wood, glue, nails, and varnish. They would not include a portion of your payroll, rent or utilities.

Net Profit

Your net profit differs from gross profit in that it includes all other business expenses, not just the direct costs. The additional expenses include costs, such as payroll, utilities and taxes.

This means your net profit is really the key. When all is said and done, you need to earn more than you've paid out in expenses so that you have some profit to... likely just reinvest in your business. If everything goes well, maybe you can use that profit to pay yourself and your team a little extra. You could buy that pinball machine you've had your eye on...

Cash Flow

Here's where the crunch comes.

Cash flow is the amount and timing of the payments you receive and the expenses that you pay. Specifically, when money is actually deposited into your bank account or given to you during an immediate transaction, we count it as an inflow in your cash flow.

When you pay for an expense and the money leaves your bank account or you pay an expense in the form of cash you have on hand, that money is counted as an outflow in your cash flow on that specific day.

Here's where things often get tricky for businesses. In the case of our example contract where we have $50,000 in revenue, let's say you will be paid in two stages of $25,000 dollars each. You send out the first invoice at the start of the contract and expect to be paid in 30 days. You send out the second invoice a month later so you're expecting that payment in 30 days from the invoice date.

Assuming that you receive the money in your hand or deposit in your bank account on the exact due date you will have a cash inflow 30 days from the start of the project and the additional $25,000 60 days after the beginning of the project. You will need to have some way to keep your business running, pay staff and expenses until you receive those payments.

That's your cash flow: the amount and the timing of the payments to and from your business.

More than ever business owners need to find ways to manage and forecast their cash flow as things can get complicated quickly.

Revenue, Profit and Cash Flow Conundrum

As you can see, revenue, profit and cash flow are closely intertwined in a business. The reason cash flow is such a key to success is really quite simple. You can't run the business on promises. You need actual money on hand to pay your bills.

As you can also see, without revenue, there IS no cash flow. Without profit, your business will experience 'death by a thousand cuts.'

So, in this book, I will be focusing on cash flow but a part of the equation is looking further upstream and making sure that your revenue and profit will supply the cash flow. I'll dive into the other two 'legs of the stool' at times. It's a fact that if you have cash flow problems today, it could be directly tied to issues in your sales pipeline that's affecting your revenue or issues that cut into your profit margin.

How Profitable Businesses Fail Everyday

Now that we've dove into the deep end and established how revenue and profit connect to cash flow, I need to drop another bomb.

Even profitable companies with plenty of revenue fail because they run out of cash. It's much more common than you think and it affects businesses across the globe.

Let me show you how this works (or doesn't work, I suppose.)

You could have a contract you've signed that will pay you a highly profitable amount, thus you are profitable on paper, and the amount is enough revenue to cover all of your expenses. Yet the customer doesn't pay when the time comes, thus, your business dies.

Let me tell you a story of how a profitable (fictional) company might hit the skids:

Jane owns a design studio and just landed their biggest job to date. They'll be making a mobile app for the local power company to help their staff track their on-site repair work. The time line is tight - something to do with the client's fiscal year - but Jane is confident they can get it delivered on time and she knows they're 'good for the money'.

With the tight time line and the staff required to handle the job, she's been pushing off other clients until this project is done – a four-month turn around. However, the job will generate enough revenue to cover five months of expenses with a nice profit margin. She's confident. They're ready to roll.

Jane breezes through the contract, anxious to dive in. It all looks good to her. She gets a little money up-front, and then is paid in four installments based on their progress and 'deliverables'.

The job starts out well. Everyone on the client side is excited, as is Janes' team. This project will not only make them some great money, but it's high profile and will 'put them on the map.'

With cash in hand from the up-front payment, the team dives into the job. Their first deliverable is a highly detailed technical plan and 'wireframe' drawings of the app. It's like the blue prints and plan for what they're going to build.

Several weeks in, they have their first meeting and present the plans. All is good. Once these plans are rubber stamped, she can invoice the next quarter of the job.

Then she gets a call. The meeting is going to be delayed a week since one of the technical advisors on the client side was pulled into a job that has her out of the office.

Ok, well, no worries. We can make up that time… but it would have been nice to invoice that first amount.

One week passes and the meeting is finally set. It's time to get things back on track.

The meeting is going well and the technical brief is right in line with what they need. The technical advisor that was off-site last week points out a critical issue in the logic. It just won't work with their system as-is. They need to do some development on their side to hook everything up but there are still a few unknowns. Give them a week to figure it out then they can meet and nail down the technical drawings.

They're another week behind, and now two weeks without sending in an invoice. This is getting tight.

As the project moves along, more and more delays take the job to a grinding halt. The four-month project is now stretching into six.

The delays mean her team is often sitting idle. She scrambles to bring in more work. Meanwhile, her business bank account is getting low. Payroll and the bills never take a break!

She lands a few smaller jobs, but can't convince the clients to pay anything up front, she's too desperate for the money to force the issue. The team is finally busy again and things are working out ok. Right?

She has contracts that will cover her for the full six months. She knows her monthly expenses, and there's plenty of money to cover the costs, leaving her with a nice profit at the end of the day. It's all good.

…but she needs to make payroll on Friday and the money isn't in her account. There's no way around it, she's writing a personal check to cover the costs and that personal check is just about bleeding her savings dry. She's worried but when she does the math, it all works out. The revenue is there and the jobs are profitable. No problem.

There is a problem. Even as the different phases of jobs are approved and she can finally send out invoices, the terms in her contracts mean she won't get paid for 30 days. Even worse, she's finding out as time moves on that the 30-day deadline isn't really a deadline at all. The payments aren't coming in and she's on the phone everyday trying to get receipt of payments owed to her.

Excuses. Promises. But no money yet.

She's finally out of cash, both in her business account and personally. Of course, she's owed a lot of money, but those invoices don't pay the bills. Time is simply up for her business.

That's how a profitable business fails. No matter how the numbers work out on paper, the business needs money on-hand to pay their bills.

Jane is a fictional person but the circumstances are intimately familiar to me. I ran a similar type of business for over a decade. I know this story well. When you multiply the number of projects, the number of invoices and the staff several times over, the issue just gets more complicated and much larger.

Fortunately, we always survived the delays, the deadbeats and the drama. Sometimes it was by the skin of our teeth.

I talk with business owners and entrepreneurs everyday. Everything generally looks pretty good from the outside. Conversations "get real," really quick and the reality spills out. Business is tough. Each day is filled with stories, challenges, barriers, wins and losses. It's amazing how often just getting paid on time is at the top of the list.

So, even though we'll explore revenue and profit from time to time in this book, the true focus is on near term cash flow. Making sure you understand the impact, the risks and the key factors that affect your business. We're going to show you how to weather the storm and grow your business.

Why Doesn't Everyone Manage Cash Flow?

It's plain to see how dangerous a cash flow crunch can be. So, why doesn't every business manage their cash flow as if their life depends on it?

Well, that's a good question. When I look back on my experience, it took a significant crisis to get my attention. Before that, I just had my head in the sand and thought I could keep ahead of the monster nipping at my ankles. It seemed like if we just worked harder, everything would work itself out in the end.

But here are a few of the reasons people fail to manage their cash flow and some misconceptions that go hand-in-hand.

1. You are afraid to know the truth.

Cash flow issues are stressful and sometimes you just don't 'want to know.' It's the feeling that somehow, knowing where you are will be worse …meanwhile, you lie awake at night.

I know from my own experience and talking with hundreds of business owners, 'knowing' is better in nearly every single way. Knowing gives you options. Knowing buys you time. Knowing helps you plan.

Imagine stepping off the curb right in front of a bus. It's game over. Now imagine stepping off the curb and looking down the block to see the bus 300 feet away. Do you step back onto the curb? Continue to cross the street? Wave down the bus so that the driver stops? You have time and options.

'Knowing' leads to more and more knowledge. You start with getting your near-term cash flow under control, but soon you're looking a few weeks forward – then a few months. At some point, it's second nature to be building revenue projections for the year and knowing how you're going to get there.

2. You don't have time.

You don't have time to manage your cash flow. Not true. You have the time. You're choosing to prioritize everything else above dealing with your cash flow.

The crazy part is that many of the things you DO prioritize are all about cash flow in a roundabout way. You're chasing down clients to try to get money in the door. You're scrambling to bring in more work, to get money coming in the door. You're working 'harder' to get things done fast and …to get money coming in the door.

You run around doing what you think is best in any particular moment but have only a gut instinct of what you really need to be doing to keep your doors open, let alone grow your business effectively.

I know what it's like – you're working hard so there couldn't possibly be another minute in the day to deal with things. However, working hard is not the same as working smart. Working on the wrong thing is terribly inefficient and bleeds time out of your day. When the things you do are reactionary, you end up just jumping from task to task, partially finishing the last one.

Imagine knowing to what part of your business you truly need to dedicate time. Understanding where you sit, why and what needs to be done to move your business forward gives you clarity, helps you delegate and take back control of your business.

Managing your cash flow doesn't 'take time' it gives you time back. Would you give an hour a week up to make back two? What about a half-hour to buy back four?

The cool thing is that you don't have to spend much time at it. In fact, likely the most efficient way to buy back your time, get some direction and move your business forward, is to get some help to manage your cash flow forecasts. Then it becomes a short conversation with your accountant or bookkeeper every week to know exactly where you're going and a short to-do list to get there.

Time-saved, knowledge gained, and operations massively improved. With an investment in time and expertise that offers you value multiple times over what you put in.

The big danger, that we see repeatedly, is in the failure to prioritize cash flow forecasting until you're up to your neck in a crisis that could cost you your business. Or at least cost you several nights sleep, add a few gray hairs to your head and result in a big bill from your accounting pro at the end of the year as they clean up the mess.

The time to get started IS when things are going well. Take the time, get your cash flow under control, set up processes and you will have much smoother sailing ahead. Spend the money now and get the system set up properly. That will not only give up-to-date info throughout the year, it will inevitably save you money at the end of the year when you have everything properly recorded and reconciled ahead of time.

3. You don't 'understand' cash flow.

We hear this comment a lot from business owners – "I don't understand cash flow [management]." Business owners rarely have a finance background out of the gate and managing cash flow seems beyond their grasp.

They're mistaken.

If you've been in business for any length of time, you know cash flow all too well. And being in business, you've proven yourself a fast learner, adaptable and willing to get your hands dirty.

The truth is that cash flow forecasting is easy to do once you have a handle on the basic principles, and once you understand the key issues your business faces, take some time to build out a simple system that works for you.

I'll admit, the 'help' out there is a little thin in this area (hence this book.) I've done the searches to see what's available for entrepreneurs. There's a never-ending number of articles, videos, business books and 'systems' that tell you how important cash flow IS to a business, but the advice seems to boil down to "use a spreadsheet." That's it. Spreadsheets solve all. But it's like telling you to use an open fire to cook with no recipe in sight. Not ideal in any sense.

There are automated systems constantly hitting the market that promise to handle your cash flow without you touching a thing. There are circumstances and business models where these can help, to a degree. But the truth is that the businesses that struggle the most with cash flow often suffer from big bills, big invoices, and constant payment and timing issues. They face factors so complicated and so 'human' that people still need to be involved to make it work.

Don't worry. We've got you covered. You'll know a ton about cash flow and exactly how to tackle it once you get through this book.

4. You don't know how to get started.

The simple answer is start small. Don't try to 'boil the ocean' and make an end-to-end 'perfect' system. You will work towards that over time, but getting started should be focused, straightforward and efficient.

Picture it this way: you're standing in a forest surrounded by trees and have no idea where to go. First, let's just get headed in the right direction. Later, you'll reach the high ground and look a little further out. Finally, you'll start to identify land-marks in the distance and plot a more accurate course.

Start with your greatest issue. The one key factor that's affect-ing your business the most. Is it getting your invoices paid on time? Having cash around to buy inventory? Scaling up fast to tackle a big job?

We'll not only help you to identify your key issues and prior-itize, we'll take that information and use it to lead you to a starting point that will get you off the ground fast.

Once you've tackled the first challenge, you'll naturally start to wonder 'what if?' That's when you can take more steps forward and move from your near term cash flow through to the coming weeks, months and how you will make your goal this year.

5. Your business is different. Cash flow isn't an issue.

Cash flow is critical for every business...

...but it is true some businesses aren't affected to the same degree by a potential cash flow crunch. In other words, they're unlikely to 'get hit by the cash flow bus.' It's more common that businesses with regular, reliable cash flow have fewer big cash flow issues, but they can end up with 'death by a thousand cuts' if they aren't profitable or don't have enough revenue. Those issues flow downhill and eventually you'll get hit.

Now, if you're reading this book I'm guessing that cash flow is a key challenge for you. But if your business falls into the category that's less affected with short-term crisis than others (we'll find out in the coming chapters) then the 'gold' in forecasting is a little different but no less valuable.

The key for businesses with regular, reliable cash flow is in understanding how to make your business more profitable, lower your risk, generate more revenue and grow. Growth is expensive though... and back to cash flow, you need it to grow.

6. It won't help me.

I can tell you from my own experience through two decades of business, along with hundreds of deep-dive conversations with business owners and finance pros, forecasting will help virtually every single business in a positive way. For many, forecasting will be an absolute game-changer.

Think of your first month in business. Your first year – the first three. Think about how much you've learned since you started and how your operations have changed. How many of those lessons were learned the hard way? Through struggle, nasty surprises and amateur mistakes?

How many of those mistakes will you make again? Likely not many since you simply know better.

Forecasting gives the 'dry run' (subtle plug!) that you need to learn and adjust before you tackle the next step for real. Forecasting gives you direction. Time to adjust. Knowledge to build on.

Of course, forecasting isn't penny perfect and it's only as good as the information you enter. But you've got more data than you know and better intuition than you think. Forecasting is often about getting all of the data in one clear picture so that you can pick up the important things. It's more of a white-board and brainstorming session that collects thoughts and identifies your options to help you pick the best direction.

7. You think you're already managing your cash flow because you read all of your financial statements.

Let's be very clear. Financial statements are the exact OPPOSITE of forecasting. They are a report on past activities. They are simply about looking in the rear-view mirror. And they should be used as much as a rear-view mirror. A look into the past offers a handful of hints that might help you pinpoint some issues in your business and discover whether you are profitable and growing.

There may be some nuggets of gold in there but the benefits are limited when diving into your operations and looking at your next steps.

In fact, past data can actually be dangerous when put into use in the wrong way. For small and medium-sized enterprises (SMEs), believing the future will follow what happened in the past is simply wrong. This year WILL be different.

Even worse, many businesses only see these reports once a year and they are often already months out of date by the time they are reviewed.

Take those nuggets of data that can help you better understand your business, but just like driving a car, focus on what's ahead of you. Forecasts need to be updated regularly and reviewed. For most businesses, a quick weekly check-in and dealing with key tasks (like following up on overdue payments) is perfect. For some businesses with regular, predictable cash flow, a monthly review will suffice (although we recommend a more frequent check-in.) Finally, for some businesses with significant cash flow challenges, a daily deep dive is needed to stay on track.

The key is to maintain the reviews through good times and bad, and take action as soon as an issue arises. After all, the best time to follow up on an overdue payment is right now.

8. Blind optimism

Many, if not most entrepreneurs are optimistic by nature. I think it's just generally a necessity. Business is incredibly hard. It's risky, filled with dramatic highs and lows, wins and losses, stress and anxiety.

Usually it takes another entrepreneur to understand how truly hard business can be. Many on the outside think it's a way to 'do what you want, when you want' and make a fortune. Easy, right? But anyone who's been in the trenches of business with their ass on the line, knows that the battle is real and, at times, nearly impossible to win.

I've had people, that understand the risks, ask me why anyone would start a business. Well, that's a good question. I usually answer in two parts. First, we're too naïve when we start to truly understand what we're getting into and by the time the "shit hits the fan", we're too far down the road to turn around.

The second, it ends up addictive, in a perverse sort of way. Why do people run marathons? Climb the most dangerous mountains in the world? Skydive? Do any number of risky, highly uncomfortable things?

I don't feel like I'm a big risk-taker. I don't skydive. Climb mountains or run marathons. (Although I'll admit to a habit of driving too fast, taking a bike down mountains that shouldn't be ridden and maybe a risky move or two on a skateboard...but I digress.)

I feel like I work hard to limit risk. In reality, I guess I have, and do, take business risks that are optimistic (although researched and carefully planned) and are tied to dire consequences if/when things go wrong.

An entrepreneur friend of mine puts it rather succinctly: "we're like dogs off a leash – we can never go back."[4] I know I'd never do anything else.

Faith, belief, luck and blind optimism don't pay the bills. The time to get started managing your cash flow is right now.

Manage Your Cash Flow, Change your Life

I'm going to restate a statistic from earlier in the book. 70% of the businesses that fail were PROFITABLE when they closed their doors. That's not by accident.

All of those businesses should have survived and thrived. They simply ran out of cash. They failed to see the problems and address them before they were hit.

Cash flow planning/management/modeling/projections/ forecasting… whatever you want to call it, is essential. It IS the difference between success and failure in the majority of cases. Cash flow management issues are the number one killer but conversely, cash flow management is the number one hero of business.

Here's why:

It's all about timing.

Since we can see that many companies that fail from cash flow problems were profitable on paper, and generally revenue wasn't the issue, it often comes down to having cash on hand to cover your costs when those expenses need to be paid. In other words, you need money in before you have to pay it out. It's all about the timing of those payments.

Picture this: It's Monday and you have payroll this Friday and need to pay all of your staff a grand total of $32,000. You have $19,500 in the bank and a $15,000 invoice that is due Tuesday. You'll have a grand total of $34,500 in the bank on Friday.

Simple right? You can keep track of that in your head!

The problem is that business is NEVER that simple. Here's an example on the following page, Fig 2:

All looks good at a glance.

Then take a look at the hidden factors in Fig 3 on the following page:

The reality is that your client hasn't processed the payment yet and unbeknownst to you, that payment won't arrive for over three weeks.

You wrote a check to a supplier three weeks ago for $2,700 in materials and they've finally just deposited the check. You thought it had already cleared. Worse, you have a $12,000 quarterly tax charge you forgot about that will clear on Tuesday.

Fig 2. Weekly Cash Flow

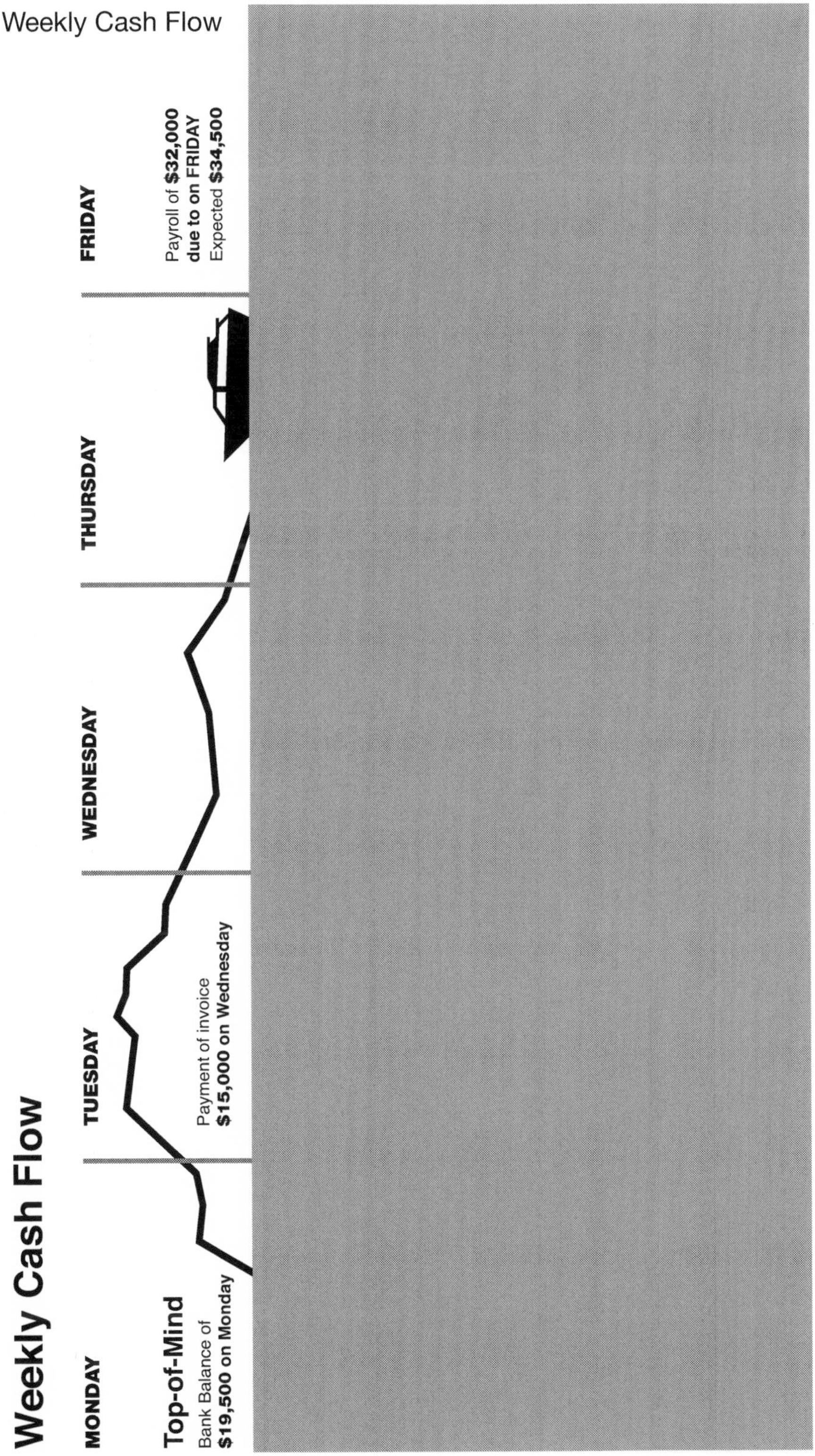

Weekly Cash Flow

Top-of-Mind

MONDAY

Bank Balance of
$19,500 on Monday

TUESDAY

Payment of invoice
$15,000 on Wednesday

WEDNESDAY

THURSDAY

FRIDAY

Payroll of **$32,000**
due to on FRIDAY
Expected **$34,500**

Weekly Cash Flow

Fig 3. Hidden Dangers

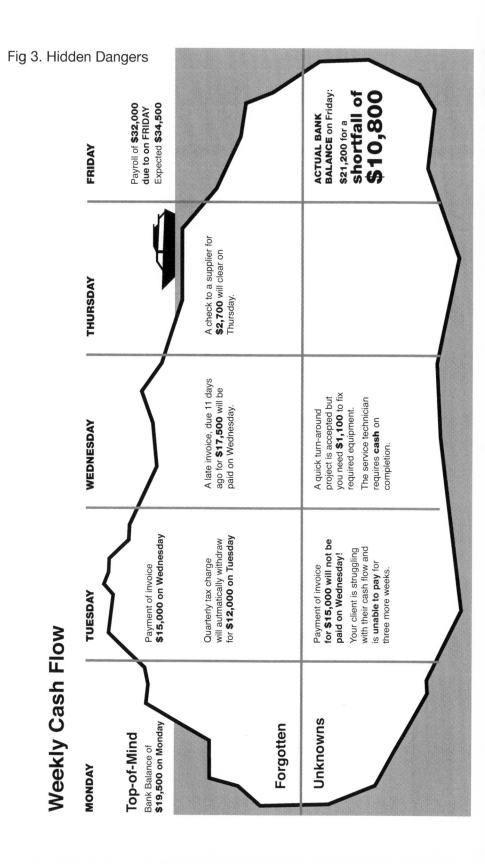

MONDAY

Top-of-Mind
Bank Balance of **$19,500 on Monday**

TUESDAY

Payment of invoice **$15,000 on Wednesday**

Quarterly tax charge will automatically withdraw for **$12,000 on Tuesday**

WEDNESDAY

A late invoice, due 11 days ago for **$17,500** will be paid on Wednesday.

THURSDAY

A check to a supplier for **$2,700** will clear on Thursday.

FRIDAY

Payroll of **$32,000 due to on FRIDAY** Expected **$34,500**

Forgotten

Unknowns

Payment of invoice for **$15,000 will not be paid on Wednesday!** Your client is struggling with their cash flow and is **unable to pay** for three more weeks.

A quick turn-around project is accepted but you need **$1,100** to fix required equipment.
The service technician requires **cash** on completion.

ACTUAL BANK BALANCE on Friday: $21,200 for a **shortfall of $10,800**

You're going to be short and absolutely scrambling on Friday to make this all work. Which, in reality, means you'll be taking money out of your personal account and putting it into your business account to cover payroll.

Even that example was laughably simple. The fact is that it's more likely that you have dozens of moving parts that are affecting your cash flow at any given time. Invoices to be paid, credit card deposits and payments, unexpected bills, automatic withdrawals, multiple bank accounts, multiple currencies… the list goes on and on.

If you dumped everything on a spreadsheet, it would look like an army of ants wandering in every direction on your screen. Even an army of 'ants' is preferable than going by your memory.

There's simply too much happening in your business at any given time to have a working understanding of every factor that will affect your cash flow.

Knowledge + Time + Action

Here's a basic formula for cash flow forecasting:

Knowledge + Time + Action = Effective Cash Flow Management

Knowledge

Knowing is key. We know that sometimes the greatest barrier to healthy cash flow is the reluctance of business owners to "know the awful truth."

That's a fleeting feeling though. If there is a cash flow problem, you WILL know…and likely very soon. So, the 'ignorance is bliss' tactic is short-lived. The business owner is rarely ignorant to the problem. Far from it. They often have intuition that tells them there's an issue looming. They lie awake at night while the cash flow monster grows bigger and bigger in their mind.

Not so much bliss in their ignorance. Is not knowing truly better than knowing? In my experience, *knowing* is nearly always less stressful.

But knowing isn't just about how you feel. Knowing that there is a problem is the first step. Understanding the scale of the problem is the second step. Problem solving is the third step.

Time

When you know about a problem is critical. Time is a massive advantage that proactive 'knowing' gives you.

Imagine that it's Wednesday and payday is Friday. You take a quick look at your bank account and there's just enough money to cover all the payments to your staff.

You write the checks and pass them out to staff on Friday as planned. By Monday, your bank calls reporting numerous bounced checks. Now you have a huge mess on your hands. You have angry staff, extra fees, and your bank is getting nervous.

It's a nasty way to find out you have a cash flow issue and it's not over yet. Your account is still empty and you still owe your staff their pay. Your bank is not likely eager to help. Hopefully you have enough cash in your personal account to lend to the business and live to fight another day.

So what happened? You look in your account and you can see an automated payment for rent was withdrawn before many of the checks had cleared. You simply didn't realize the dates would overlap.

You've learned the biggest risk factor in cash flow. Timing.

So let's look at the situation from a different point of view. One where you're forecasting your cash flow and keeping careful track of timing of all of those inflows and outflows of cash.

It's Monday morning, three weeks prior, and your bookkeeper has just reconciled your file. There seems to be a problem and she's highlighting it in your regular Monday cash flow report.

From what she can see, you will be short of cash in three weeks and won't be able to make payroll.

She flags three invoices as the culprits. They're not expected to be in for over a week after the shortfall, and that's only IF they come in on time.

She hops on the phone with you to discuss. Here's where cash flow forecasting moves from science to an art. It's all in the action you take.

Action

To illustrate the benefit of giving yourself time to act versus an immediate and unexpected shortfall, let's look at some potential options to dealing with the previous example.

In your conversation with your bookkeeper, a few options float to the top. You can talk to your bank and see if they can offer some short-term relief through a line of credit of loan. The key thing to recognize here is that banks are highly risk-averse.

So, walking in and saying "I need cash by Friday" will likely get you shown to the door in short order.

If you talk to your banker three weeks out, show her the forecast that demonstrates you're likely to be back in the black within a couple of weeks. If you show your expected inflows of cash alongside a sales report that reveals the shortfall to be a rare and temporary 'blip' in your cash flow, the bank will be more likely to believe that short-term financing is low risk and help you out of the jam.

With time on your side, there may be other options to consider. You can try to accelerate payment of one of the outstanding invoices, two of which are large enough to cover the shortfall. This is where the 'art of business' comes in. In reality, it's often about relationships you have with your clients (but that's another topic). Keep in mind, that these conversations have the potential to be of concern to your clients so before you begin these conversations, weigh the risks.

To take action, you get on the phone with the three clients that have invoices sitting on their desks. Now there are likely a couple of options here. First, simply ask your clients if they are willing to speed up payment by a week. If you have a good relationship with your clients this works more often than you might think.

Where I've found it less effective is when the client organization is big enough to have finance and legal departments. They often like to stick to the letter-of-the-law. So, tactic number two is to offer a small discount for early payment. Hopefully small enough that you don't completely erode your profit but, in this case, the situation is too serious and cash flow trumps all.

There may be other options to work with the client and speed up payment. Think outside the box. Could early delivery of a later deliverable be traded for quicker payment? Reducing the price of a later phase? Adding some additional service or products to a later deliverable for a reduced rate? Conversations are key. Let me digress with a quick note here: Conversations in person OR on the phone. Email is not a good option for these types of requests and negotiations.

You can review the cash flow situation with your bookkeeper and see if there are any payables from your side that can be delayed. Are you paying any of your bills early? Has everything your suppliers promised arrived in good order? Explore all of the outgoing cash and see if there's an opportunity to delay payment. Of course, I never recommend paying your bills late. That is most likely to harm your business, either in the near term, or over the long haul.

Similar to requesting early payment from a client, you may see an opportunity to negotiate late payment with a supplier. You might be able to make an offer that will allow you to push back the due date of a bill. Likewise to discussing payment timing with clients, discussing these issues with your suppliers could potentially lower their confidence in your business moving forward. Consider this option carefully before proceeding with these conversations.

There are other options for short-term relief. If you are able, simply covering the shortfall personally may be your best option. Personal loans from friends or family, investment into your business, selling equipment that's no longer required, selling inventory at a discount with payment up-front, a quick-turnaround project with 'on-delivery' payment terms. There may be some expenses you could cut before the required payment hits.

The list goes on.

I've listed around a dozen potential options for short-term cash flow relief to demonstrate the importance of giving yourself time. The key to nearly every single option is that you need TIME to execute. Nearly all of these options require plenty of time to get into place before your shortfall. The more time the better.

Your Forecast as a Living Plan

By now, you've likely realized that your cash flow forecast isn't just for you. First, an accounting pro can be a trusted sounding board and advisor. Not only can they take many tasks off your shoulders, such as setting up your systems, ensuring automated data entry is flowing, and reconciling your accounts, they can ensure the data in your forecasts is up-to-date and accurate.

They serve as an early-warning system and help you focus on the key actions you need to regain control of your cash flow.

Your forecast helps you to identify all of the different options you have at hand and what path might make the most sense, at least this time-around.

Taking a step back, you can see that your cash flow plan is likely a requirement from your bank to consider any sort of short-term relief. Likewise, your forecasts may be required to undertake many of the other options for the lenders and investors, or for you to best execute your plan.

The further out the plan looks, the better. Although forecasts will inevitably grow less and less accurate the further into the future they stretch, they are essential nonetheless.

Your most effective cash flow forecast likely includes both a near term cash flow forecast alongside a revenue forecast to not only predict 'this week and this month' but also how you will reach your goal this year. Likewise, lenders and investors want to see further out as well. We'll get into more detail in this area in later chapters.

Maintaining up-to-date cash flow and sales forecasts, and reviewing them weekly at a minimum, is essential for buying yourself time, keeping your options open and getting help. It's the first and most essential step in lowering your risk and growing your business.

Ten Factors that Affect Business Cash Flow

Before we dive into a system and process for managing your cash flow, we're going to take a deep dive on ten factors that are often the culprit in cash flow shortfalls.

These sections all relate to the Cash Flow Scorecard in Appendix A at the end of this book. A downloadable version of the scorecard is also available at pandemiccashflow.com. If you're a business owner I recommend working your way through the score card to help you identify factors that may have the greatest affect on your cash flow. If you are an accounting pro, you may want to use this score card as a talking point with your clients

Looking into each issue in a little bit of depth will give you a greater understanding of the problems and help you to identify your key issues.

Once you have a better understanding of the issues, we'll dive into a system and process for managing your cash flow.

1. Payment Method

The payment type of individual purchases can have a significant effect on your cash flow. The lowest risk being cash payments, since you have the cash on hand immediately. It's important to note that although the risk may be lower in this case, the danger of a shortfall is real and can be devastating to a business.

Often, in cash sales, shortfalls occur when sales drop below the break-even point and the business has failed to keep cash on hand to deal with just such an issue. A drop in sales may be seasonal or related to other unanticipated problems such as growing competition.

Whatever the issue, it's critical to maintain cash on hand, track key performance indicators (KPIs) and forecast the coming months to keep a tight grip on your cash flow.

Conversely, the highest risk payment type consists of invoices paid later, since you don't have the cash on hand to pay bills. Not only are you forced to await payment, you're relying on your customer to pay their bills on time (or at all!) Unfortunately, invoices are just an unpleasant fact in business. When payments are large, they simply aren't often paid in cash, customers want detailed documentation, and often delivery of the product or service prior to paying.

In fact, often the greatest strain on cash flow is a result of late payments on big invoices. More on this later...

2. The Size of Your Individual Sales

The average size of your customers' purchases can have a significant effect on your cash flow. Numerous, smaller purchases can lower your risk since your cash flow is spread out over a larger number of transactions and losing a single sale will have a lower impact on your business than a large transaction. Of course, attracting a high volume of customers presents its own set of challenges.

In the case of small purchases in high volume, it's critical to identify key factors that could affect your overall sales, such as a reduction in repeat sales, loss of a segment of customers, or an overall reduction of individual sales. Dropping daily revenue is a warning sign but uncovering the underlying issues that lead to a drop in sales is critical in order to address the problem.

Conversely, when you have fewer clients but the individual deals are a much larger amount, your cash flow can be a greater risk of an unexpected shortfall when you lose a sale or the customer fails to pay their invoice. These types of shortfalls are often large, dramatic and stressful.

The number of customers, tied with the size of individual sales is likely a consequence of your business model and to some degree, unlikely to change. However, it's prudent to understand the risk you face and evaluate whether you can make some slight adjustments to ensure that you aren't completely dependent on a customer or two to survive.

To be clear, I'm not suggesting that one business model or the other is a better bet. We're just focusing on cash flow risk here. However, there is some potential wisdom in the comparison. If the majority of your business right now is spread among several large clients, paying infrequent but large sums, you may want to consider options to diversify your cash flow.

Can you increase the number of payments by splitting the large sums up into more frequent, smaller payments? Doing so could help you smooth out your cash flow and lower the risk of a shortfall if a large invoice fails to be paid.

Are there possible services or products that you could offer to a wider range of customers, in smaller amounts, to help broaden your customer base and keep cash flowing in?

Is there an opportunity to split off part of your services or deliverables into immediate cash payments as part of your existing jobs? For instance, can you get an upfront payment that's immediate to kick off a project? Alternatively, ask for immediate payment to cover hard costs on delivery, installation, or service calls?

Understanding the risks for both ends of the spectrum is critical so that you are tracking the right data and staying on top of your cash flow. Although fewer, larger deals can have a nearly immediate and dramatic impact on your cash flow, it's important to track trends in your cash flow when your business is powered through numerous, smaller transactions.

3. The Scourge of Late Payments

Late payments are simply the number one and often the most frustrating reason for cash flow shortfalls and thus, the number one reason businesses fail. Late payments are chronic and debilitating. One study revealed that, on average, construction companies in the region suffered from over $220,000 in outstanding receivables (60+ days overdue) at any given time.[5]

Talking to business owners around the globe on a daily basis, we know that late payments are the norm nearly everywhere. Of course, as we've shown in the previous factors, overdue payments affect some business models more than others. Specifically, the ones that invoice then await payment.

If your business is routinely affected by late paying customers, it's essential that you keep very careful track of your cash flow and stay on top of overdue payments.

Staying on top of late payments is critical. Getting those late payments often involves simply staying in frequent contact with your customer. Follow up on overdue items immediately. The sooner you talk to the customer, the more they realize you are serious about being paid on time. Of course, handle the conversation carefully and professionally. Relationship building is critical. Anger will most likely result in an even later payment.

Make sure you stay on top of the late items and follow up weekly. The longer a payment sits, the more likely it is that you will not receive the full amount, or even worse, the customer may simply refuse to pay. Frequent contact, even when handled in a polite and professional manner, will likely move things along. It's been proven repeatedly, that the 'squeaky wheel gets the grease.'

Often, negotiation before a contract is signed, changes to the payment terms and adding in potential penalties are simply the easiest way to speed up payments. There are numerous ways you may be able to speed up payments to your business and worth every minute and penny to implement.

In fact, the issue is so big that, at the end of the book, you'll see an entire guide to getting paid faster in Appendix B and a payment checklist in Appendix C to help you minimize late payments. Both documents are also available for download at pandemiccashflow.com.

4. Your Budget is the Bottom Line

The size of your monthly recurring budget relates directly to the amount of cash you need to have on hand to feed the business and keep it moving forward. The business model itself is often the largest factor in the size of your ongoing expenses. Some businesses have much higher overhead than others and a large portion of the expenses are just the cost of doing business.

For instance, a manufacturing business is likely to have costly equipment and the need for significant floor space to build and warehouse their products. An engineering firm will likely have significant expenses in their human resources, while a high-end retail store may be spending a large portion of their budget on rent in a prime location.

Seasonal businesses may have low expenses during a portion of the year, but of course, also low income during the same period. A film producer may have very low overhead month to month while they are between projects, but very heavy expenses that need to be tracked carefully during productions.

It's important to recognize how your recurring budget affects your cash flow in your business. How long you can go during lean months and still keep your doors open and how quickly you can scale back expenses during a lean time.

It's also essential for virtually every business to evaluate on an ongoing basis which expenses are critical for their operations and growth but also evaluate costs that are not giving you the return on investment for your precious cash.

Start by maintaining a detailed running budget then review and update the budget on a quarterly basis, when costs are expected to change, or when you are planning an expansion. When you are adding expenses, especially large, ongoing costs, carefully review the terms and seek ways to reduce or eliminate the new costs if crisis arises.

Investigate and understand the effectiveness and return on investment that your greatest costs deliver and act immediately and accordingly rather than waiting for crisis to hit.

There is one other type of forecast and plan that can be a lifesaver for nearly any business when crisis hits. It's called a 'lean budget plan.'

Essentially, a lean budget plan is exactly as it sounds. It's a budget that you keep filed away and update quarterly. This plan strips out anything in your budget that is not essential to maintain operations. It's a worst-case scenario plan and it's great to have on hand if the worst case strikes. You can take action fast.

5. The Breakdown of Your Largest Costs

Expenses range from small, cash purchases through to large bills that land on your desk and are due at a later date. The larger a single expense is, the greater the immediate impact it will have on your cash flow. A big bill that arrives, 'due upon receipt,' can be the most dangerous hit to your cash flow, especially if you aren't keeping careful track of your inflows and outflows of cash.

Smaller, cash payments do take cash out of your hand immediately, but you will have a better idea of where your cash flow stands and it can keep you 'honest' with yourself. Large bills, when they are not tracked properly, often appear unexpectedly and demand immediate attention.

Bills that are due later, for instance in thirty days, do give you a little room to move and potentially some time to manage your money to ensure the cash is available when you need it. Bills due at a later date are so often overlooked or forgotten about until they arrive at the due date, that they can create a crisis if they aren't carefully tracked and prepared for.

You can see that the risk factors from small cash payments through to large bills all carry risk and can lead to shortfalls but at different times and for different reasons. Overall, the larger the payment, more unexpected it is, and the shorter the time frame to pay the bill, the greater the risk. However, it's critical to stay on top of all of your expenses and keep track of the timing of the inflows and outflows of money so that you are prepared to pay the expenses when the time comes.

Dealing with big bills may be softened with a little bit of pre-planning and negotiation. If possible, split up the costs into smaller, more frequent payments over time, rather than fewer, larger expenses.

Although bills that need to be paid at a later date need to be carefully tracked, ensure that you are paying them on-time but not early. Paying bills early may help you keep track of your overall cash balance, it can be a dangerous practice if you do not track your cash flow carefully as you could create a shortfall by paying out cash before it's necessary. Of course, if you are tracking your cash flow carefully, then there is virtually no benefit to paying bills early.

6. Paying Your Bills Past their Due Date

Often the number one tactic, and sometimes the only alternative for a business to survive a shortfall, is to pay some of their bills late. The bills that are paid late are often viewed as less essential to keeping the business afloat, and, at times, that's true. Sometimes bills simply need to be paid late in order to prevent your business from closure, but rest assured, paying any bills late will have a negative effect on your business.

Chronically paying your bills late often points to underlying issues in your business. It may feel like you are keeping the cash on hand and that it's a safer bet for your business, but as pressure builds to pay those overdue bills, the timing can get even more inconvenient and it often just delays a crisis, if not leading to one outright. Poor financial management often goes hand-in-hand with late payments.

Paying your bills late also hurts your reputation and thus, your business. Talking with business owners on a daily basis, we hear first-hand how damaging late payments can be. Delaying payment to a supplier or contractor late might feel like a short term win for you but you may be putting your payee in a horrible situation. Possibly even driving them out of business.

Tragically, late payments often hit an entire 'food chain' of businesses. Here's an example of how this can happen:

An organization leading a large project delays payment to a supplier, who owes money to their own contractor, and that contractor has materials costs to pay off. The supplier is unable (or refuses) to pay the contractor until they get their money from the project lead. Likewise the contractor is in a bind, unable to pay their materials bill. It ends up a chain of missed payments, shortfalls and crisis.

I've seen this too many times to not mention it. In fact, I've been a victim of it myself, in the past. Unfortunately, it isn't a rarity and the ramifications flow all the way down the chain. No matter the reason for withholding payment, the negative waves and shortfalls can hit a number of businesses affecting dozens, sometimes hundreds of people.

Most importantly, if you are withholding payment from a supplier or contractor for even a legitimate reason, do not take it lightly. It could have wide-ranging negative affects that you may be completely unaware of.

Hearing and experiencing these sorts of payment issues over decades of business, I can tell you that late payments rarely go unpunished; often in ways the offender may not even be aware.

Business is still most often built on relationships, particularly when large sums of money and 'pay later' terms are involved. That's just part of doing business. That also means conversations between all the parties involved are likely frequent, truths are often revealed and even the smallest business, at the end of the food chain can have an impact up the ladder.

Late payments can lead to late fees, late deliverables, fired clients, price increases on future work, refusal of the contractors and suppliers to even bid on a job. And often the best contractors and suppliers are not lacking for work, which means they have little trouble skipping bids offered by less-than-reliable businesses.

Rest assured that a history of late payments may not only affect your business negatively, but in the end, could even spell its demise.

When the inevitable hits and you simply can't afford to pay a bill on time, let your payee know as soon as possible. Apologize; take responsibility for the delay and outline when you will be able to pay. If paying a portion is possible, do so. It will go a long way to reassuring your supplier and easing their own cash flow situation.

7. The Paradox of Fast Growth

Growth is critical for businesses to gain traction and create economies of scale that can lead to greater profit, but growing too fast has been the root cause of many business failures. It can lead to the tragic cash flow crunch that, in the end, serves as the death knell for a business. Growth is expensive, even at a steady rate and will certainly be a big hit on your cash flow.

Nearly static growth may carry the lowest risk to your cash flow, but while that may be true in the simplest of terms, static growth is not a path to success. Static growth, or worse contraction, may not be as likely to land you in a major cash flow crunch in the immediate term but it can be a slow, grueling death for a business. Growth is critical for continued business success and in the bigger picture, should provide much more cash flow than you experienced pre-growth if all of the puzzle pieces come together.

Stable growth requires that you understand where all of your key numbers sit. Has your revenue been growing and is it projected to continue to grow? Is your profit margin solid and expected to increase with expansion? Is cash rolling in and helping you to establish some savings?

It's critical that you truly understand your current state of growth and build highly realistic projections of where growth can take your business so that you make informed decisions.

8. Funding Your Growth

As we've already discussed, growth is critical for business, but expenses are sure to go up. Your staff expect pay raises, competitors are constantly creating efficiencies that affects pricing and innovation is key in nearly any industry to remain competitive. That all takes money.

Simply put, if you're not growing, you're floundering. Trying to break-even is not a goal. You're going to land on one side of the fence or the other. Growth is expensive, complicated and fraught with risk. There are so many unknowns in growth, no matter how well laid out the plan. Costs usually out pace estimates and it takes longer than you could have expected. At least that's what you need to be prepared for to make sure expansion goes as smooth as possible.

Not only is growth expensive, it can hamper productivity and efficiency for all sorts of reasons: new staff that need to be trained, moving operations to a new location, set-up of new equipment, increased client loads that often are the impetus for growth – and the list goes on.

Each of these factors can have a major effect on your cash flow. More cash is needed for growth, likely significantly more. As new demands drop into your lap threatening to halt expansion, your cash becomes the pinch point in your growth. Adding to an already complicated set of circumstance, your cash is still needed to maintain your current operations to keep things rolling.

So planning for growth is an essential task to undertake. Exploring all sorts of 'what if' scenarios, best case, worst case, likely case and understanding the money that's required for nearly any eventuality.

This highly complicated set of circumstances leads us to explore the way you're planning to fund your growth. With such a highly complicated set of circumstances, the answer isn't as obvious as it appears.

As far as cash flow danger goes, in the end, you need to have enough capital on hand to fund your growth, cover operations and have a significant 'war-chest' of cash for all the unexpected, worst case scenarios that could appear.

There may be circumstances when funding growth through cash flow is your best bet, other times, outside capital such as debt or investment might be the strongest move for your business. The key is to truly understand your circumstances, evaluate all of your options and make an informed decision. Let's peek at a couple of the options.

The principal reason that funding growth through cash on-hand is that debt is expensive. A significant portion of your loan will likely go to paying 'itself' back, at least in the near term. There's also interest attached to the loan, which can make the capital costly and could hurt you in the end.

However, the principal reason that funding growth through cash may lower your risk, is that you may still have the option of accessing capital through debt if or when the need comes up. Think of it as a safety net that, although not guaranteed to be available, it may be available if you need it. Conversely, funding expansion through a loan leaves you little room for error.

However, for you, debt may be the best strategy. Taking on a loan to fuel your growth while maintaining solid cash reserves could be the best option for your business. For some, the only path to growth is via outside capital and approaching growth too conservatively, could be a much riskier path.

The most likely case is that you will fuel your growth through a combination of your own cash, debt, investment, grants and personal cash. I think it's critical that the path to growth is carefully mapped out, all of the options explored and a well-planned approach that you can execute with the least disruption to your operations and the lowest risk to your business.

As you can see, growth can be risky, complicated and unsettling. It's prudent to over-plan, forecast a range of possibilities, ask for professional advice and opinions on your plan, and expect the unexpected.

When you build your budget and cash flow forecasts that will drive your growth, stay on top of them with frequent updates to ensure that you are prepared for the unexpected factors that are sure to pop up.

Although you may not have enough capital on hand to handle the potential worst-case scenario, understand it, watch for signs that things might be heading that way and be proactive when you see signs that things may be going wrong.

9. The Importance of a War Chest

Savings give you a safety net and the more cash you have on-hand, the lower your risk of a shortfall. Building up a large nest egg of savings is really tough for most businesses, especially ones on an aggressive growth map.

We've already covered some of the dangers and risks involved in taking on debt to feed your cash flow, so I won't spend more time on that topic, but I do want to explore savings in a little more depth.

From a cash flow perspective, having ample cash on hand does lower your risk of a cash flow crunch, but that certainly doesn't mean that it's the best approach for your business. Cash that is just sitting idle in a bank account is doing little for your business, outside of serving as a potential safety net. If you do find yourself in the enviable position of running a highly profitable business and having a significant amount of cash on hand that is growing, you may want to explore your options for putting that money to use.

Is it a good time to expand? Will expansion enable you to increase your revenue, maintain or grow your profit and generate even more cash? As we've already covered, growth is expensive and needs to be carefully planned but when you have ample cash on hand, you may want to explore plans for growth.

There are other ways to put that money to work for you, outside of the obvious move to distribute some of that cash among your shareholders. You may want to consider investing the money. If you do choose to invest a portion of your cash reserves, it may be prudent to ensure that the money is easily accessible should the need arise.

Truly understanding your cash position is more than looking in your bank account on a given day. It's critical to understand how the inflows and outflows of cash will affect your cash reserves in the coming weeks and months. What appears to be a large reserve of cash could be depleted in short order with the arrival of a large bill that you've overlooked, or the need for funds to cover equipment repairs that appear unexpectedly.

10. In the End Paying Yourself is the Goal

First, if you've never missed paying yourself, especially in the early days of establishing a business or at times of growth, you're in rare company. Unfortunately, business is expensive, risky and it's often unavoidable.

Taking money from your personal savings can be extremely stressful and discouraging. The personal equation can be even more stressful if you have a spouse, partner or dependents in the equation.

If you are unable to pay yourself on a regular basis, it can be a clear sign that there are issues in your operations, which are draining your cash flow. These issues may be related to any of the previous nine factors or even related to a shortfall in revenue or a failure to generate profit. In any case, it's not an ideal situation.

I've listed this factor last, since it's less a sign that you're not familiar with and more of a wakeup call to pay special attention to your cash flow and right the ship.

If you are unable to pay yourself on a regular basis or even more extreme, constantly investing money into your business to keep it afloat, you are in a very risky situation. (But you are not alone.) Take action today and build a clear picture of your business budget and cash flow. That plan will help you take the necessary steps to plug the leaks and take control of your business.

Part 2

Implementing a Solution

5

A Bird's Eye View of an Effective Forecast

More than Accounts Payable and Receivable

We've seen how rare it is for businesses to forecast their cash flow, even though the risk is extreme and the payoff is huge for a small investment in time. We also know that time and complexity are two major barriers to building usable, up-to-date and actionable forecasts.

I know the feeling. I was in the same boat until I had no choice but to gain control of our cash flow or shut down the business. It took me some time and trial and error to build systems on spreadsheets that would help me identify key issues at a glance. Those early forecasts served as the foundation for my system, and eventually, Dryrun (our cash flow forecasting and modeling tool.)

The barriers you face are the same one's I did, so I know that you don't have a lot of time to dedicate to forecasting and the time you do put into the models better give you the insight you need to take action.

I set out to take control of my cash flow in a system that would be most logical to me, the business owner. A system that would serve as a foundation and a reference that was forward-looking and operational. I took a systematic approach to learn about my business, take action on the biggest issues I faced in the moment, but then build on that system to gain more and more insight and look farther into the future.

I'm going to walk you through processes and a system that will help you set up your foundation, learn the structure of a basic cash flow forecast, then set you free to move forward and build forecasts tailor-made for your business.

I've also made this system straightforward, intuitive and structured. This will not only help the business owner understand where they sit but also ensure that other stakeholders are on the same page and speaking the same language.

A Birds Eye View of a Basic Cash Flow Forecast

Let's take a look at the main steps in a basic cash flow forecast before we explore each in detail.

Step 1: Your Regular, Recurring Budget

A regular, recurring budget is the place to start. Building a recurring budget gives you a foundation to your finances providing a clear picture of the amount of cash you need each month to cover your base costs and stay in business. In simple terms, it helps you to have a 'break-even' point in your mind.

Automating this budget will save you a ton of setup time and minimizes updates required to keep it current. Your budget serves as a great reference for where your money is going month to month. It will help you set revenue goals and serves as a foundation to build 'what ifs' as you plan for growth.

Setting up a clear, repeating budget helps you to not only grasp the money you need to generate and the cash you need on hand from month to month, it also lets you focus on the big bills that need to be dealt with on a regular basis.

Step 2: The Bills that Sit Outside Your Recurring Budget Needs

By separating 'one-time' or irregular bills out from the regular budget, you can better keep track of 'exceptions' that need to be paid. These bills are usually paid at a later day, such as 30 days after they've been issued ('net 30'.)

Viewing these bills on a time line, separate from your regular budget, helps you to keep track of these items that are more likely to cause you grief.

Of course there are some exceptions to the rule, in the form of bills that might 'straddle the line'. For instance, you may have some regular, recurring items that need to be paid via check every month so you may want to track them separately to ensure they're not missed.

Generally, 90% of your forecast will be drop into the various sections with little thought, while the other 10% will take some decisions and customization to make sure that you're setting up a forecast that works best for you. We'll explore some of those factors in more detail in the coming chapters.

Step 3: Your Income, and Most Importantly, Who Owes you Money!

Now that you've got a handle on the money you need to pay and when, it's time to track the cash coming into your business that will pay all of those expenses and leave you some profit to help you grow.

As you saw in the cash flow overview, the highest level of risk in your income happens when you send out large invoices and have to await payment. Therefore, tracking each of these invoices by the date that you expect the cash to be in-hand is critical. You need to predict when you realistically believe the cash to arrive in your bank account. Unfortunately, too often, that is not on the due date but later, sometimes, much later.

Conversely, if your revenue is steady, cash-based sales with lots of smaller purchases, you are better off tracking daily or weekly sales rather than attempting to track every single sale. You'll just end up with information overload.

Step 4: Viewing Your Forecast as a Whole

Once you have a repeating budget in place and are tracking your 'one-time' bills and your invoices or income, it's time to take a step back and look at the entire picture. This is where you'll discover potential shortfalls that you will need to deal with.

Step 5: Moving Beyond Short-term Cash Flow

Once your near-term cash flow is under control, there is a wealth of information that can help you move your business forward. Financial forecasting for your business is often about frequency and current needs.

I like to think of it in terms of 'this week, this month and this year.' 'This week' is highly operational, near term management. With consistent, regular tracking, your chances of hitting a crisis is significantly less and you can stay on top of key items, such as overdue invoices that you need to follow-up on to make sure they don't fall through the cracks and get missed.

'This month' is a bit broader picture to make sure that you'll have the money on hand to cover your costs going forward and predict ahead of time that you are cash flow healthy several weeks out. Of course, 'this month' isn't to the day. I actually view this as a 4-6 week, even an 8-week view of the future.

'This year' is all about reaching your goals and growing your business. If you need to "make two million dollars" this year, you need to do it in twelve months, not fourteen. This concept is about building revenue forecasts that help you plot your goals, and spot potential issues well ahead of time, as well as planning for growth. When we're talking about growth planning, of course, that can stretch well beyond the one-year mark but I find it useful to picture forecasting in this sort of frequency.

Minimize Risk While Discovering Opportunity

Forecasts are not only about avoiding a crisis or dealing with a cash flow shortfall, there's more in the numbers than that. Of course, reducing your risk is critical for business survival and the first step in taking control of your cash flow, but your forecasts offer much more useful data. Data that you need to identify opportunities and make decisions that will help you grow your business. (Fig. 4 & 5)

Fig 4. Risks Identified Through Forecasting

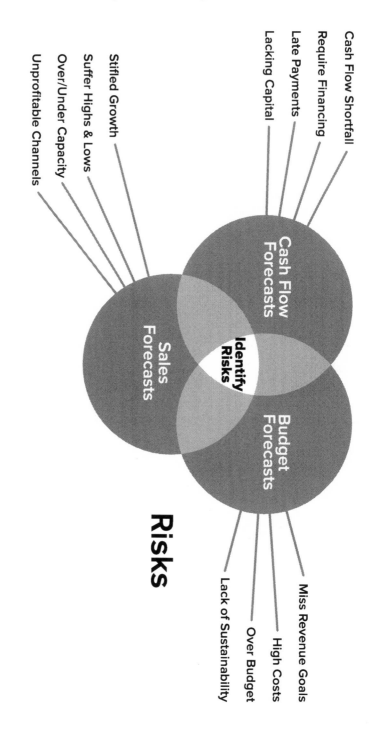

Fig 5. Opportunities Identified Through Forecasting

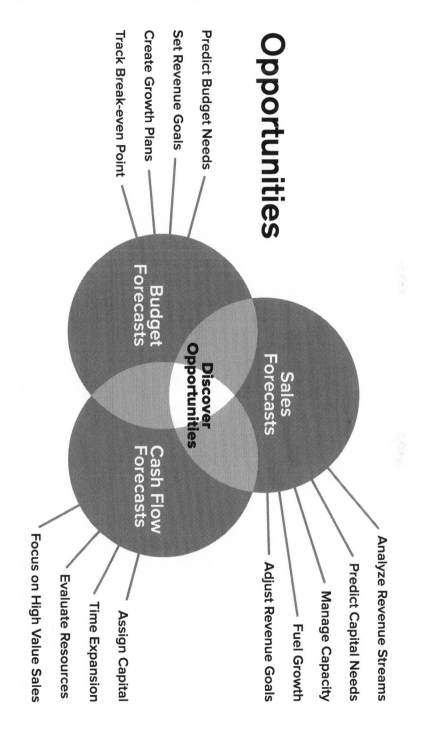

6

An Overview of the Aspects of Forecasting

Let's look at this basic concept from another perspective. Regular, consistent forecasting offers benefits, which I refer to as the pillars of forecasting. The basic benefits include:

1. Crisis Management:

Dealing with the current cash flow crisis is often the first time that business owners dive into forecasting. Unfortunately, this is the wrong time to begin the task. If you're in a state of crisis, you have no choice. Make no mistake, knowing exactly where you stand and understanding the crisis is better than following your fear and refusing to take a close look at the situation. Knowing what's going on in detail may reveal options you didn't realize existed.

The truth is, however, businesses that wait until crisis hits before trying to truly understand their situation, often leads to business death because it's simply too late and they're out of

Fig 6. The Pillars of Forecasting

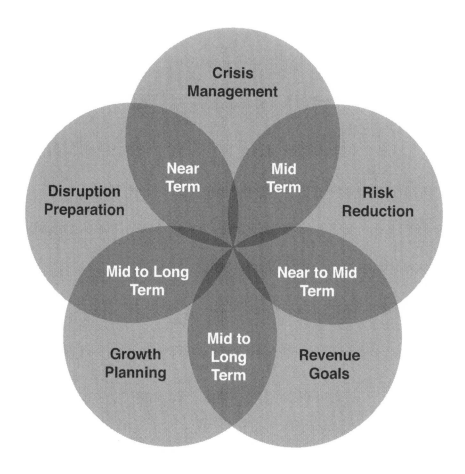

Near Term: Cash Flow Forecasts
Mid Term: Sales Forecasts
Long Term: Budget Planning

options. At that point, an understanding of the current state may at least help reduce the damage somewhat.

That's why it's critical to reduce your risk ahead of time...

2. Risk Reduction:

Consistent cash flow tracking is essential for reducing your risk of a crisis and giving yourself time and options for dealing with a potential problem.

If you're a business owner, here's where I reinforce your need for a professional to maintain your system, reconcile and clean your data, and stay on top of your cash flow forecasts, either internally or externally. We'll get into this recommendation in more detail in later chapters, but the health of your business, your efficiency, productivity, and your sleep patterns can all benefit greatly from engaging the right professional to help.

3. Exceeding Your Revenue Goals:

Once you have your ongoing, consistent forecasts keeping you on top of your cash flow, identifying and dealing with potential crisis and reducing your risk, you need to turn attention to the longer term.

A near term cash flow crisis can be a crushing unexpected blow to your business, killing it in an instant. But the root causes can vary. Often it's a result of a broken sales process that isn't driving your sales to the levels you need to break even and provide a profit. Simply put, if you don't have enough revenue you won't have enough cash flow. (I'll refer to any revenue coming into business or organization as 'sales' but it really covers any sort of income from sales to customers through to donations to a non-profit organization.) Further, if your sales fail to generate a profit, your cash flow will dwindle and your business will eventually die.

So, once your near-term cash flow is under control, it's time to look a little further ahead and understand the mid to long-term view of your sales. This task is particularly important if your business relies on landing new projects or big 'deals', rather than having regular, recurring income.

If you are dependent on 'landing that next big deal' to keep your business afloat, it's critical that you build sales forecasts that can help you stay on top of your revenue. A long list of deals won't cut it. By building realistic forecasts that track individual deals and the likelihood they will close, you will better understand where you sit for the coming twelve months and beyond.

You will be able to better identify potential slow periods as well as times when you may be overwhelmed and above your capacity to deliver. Both situations can be deadly to a business. Slow periods mean slow revenue and slow cash flow. Busy times can be painful as well. If you need to pay overtime and hire contractors to deliver during busy times, you may have ample revenue but eat up your profit margin with the additional costs.

Often a busy time coincides with a failure to keep up in generating new sales, especially when the business owners handle much of the sales. The chronic highs and lows in sales are often a result of a failure to manage a sales cycle properly.

Knowing well ahead of time what your sales will look like in the mid to long-term can give you the knowledge you need to address the problems. Increasing sales and seeking quick turnaround jobs when a slow period is looming, while negotiating varied delivery dates, refusing jobs with less-than-perfect clients or expanding your capacity ahead of time can help you deal with overwhelming capacity issues.

4. Growth Planning:

Growth is important for a healthy business. If you aren't growing your sales, and you're not generating a profit, your business is contracting, and that's deadly. Trying to break-even is folly. It's better to manage your business to a profit.

Growth is also one of the most dangerous times for a business when it's not clearly planned and properly capitalized. Forecasting your revenue, understanding the future state of your business and finances, is key to understanding when and how to grow.

Seeing a potential high in sales on the horizon can lead to planned expansion when viewed in isolation. It's critical that expansion costs be carefully plotted alongside your sales forecasts. Build 'what if' scenarios to explore as many of the potential outcomes and risks as you can imagine so that you are diving into expansion with your eyes wide open and plenty of cash on hand to manage the growth.

5. Disruption Preparation:

Unlike the other four pillars, disruption is the 'wild card' that can affect your business at any stage of forecasting. Disruption can come in many forms and often the affect disruption has on cash flow is overlooked. It can come from expansion, staff turnover, major purchases, market changes... nearly anything that will have an affect on your business overall will likely affect your cash flow.

Tackling disruption is as often as straight forward as discussing any changes expected to hit your business in the coming weeks and months in terms of the financial ramifications.

Now that you have a birds-eye view of forecasting, let's dive into these topics in a little more detail.

Your Financial Foundation:
A Regular, Recurring Budget

One of the questions that prevents business owners from getting started on a cash flow process that could save their business and power their growth, is simply not knowing where to start. It can feel like a monumental task and, when you have 500 to-dos on your list, cash flow forecasting tends to fall to the bottom... until you can feel a crisis about to hit and try to get started at 3:00 in the morning when you can't sleep.

I'm going to walk you through the process and system that I recommend to get you started as well as setting up processes that are time saving and simple to follow so that you're consistent with your forecasts.

The first question I want you to ask yourself is simply "how much does it cost for me to stay in business every month?" We're not looking for a penny perfect prediction; of course, a forecast will never be penny-perfect, not even close. That's ok, we want direction, insight and the power to make decisions. Pennies don't matter in that case.

Let's take this a step further and give it some structure. If you have a budget already made, grab it – it will save you time as we supercharge it. If you don't have a budget in some form, that's ok, we'll work our way through the process.

We're going to start the process by building a baseline, repeating budget that will serve four key purposes:

1. The budget helps you grasp your 'break-even point' so that you have a foundation to set revenue goals and understand the base cash flow you need every month.

2. To serve as an up-to-date reference point so that you have a single place to go to find out exactly what you're paying for various costs in your business and to model out changes, such as growth plans.

3. By auto-repeating the budget, you will be able to look into the future, predict your cash flow and revenue needs throughout the year. Use it as a living document constantly updating it with potential changes and 'what if' scenarios to cover all your bases.

4. The timing of these budget items is useful for understanding how your cash flow will look in the near future. Set the repeat dates for items in your budget as accurately as possible.

For instance, if you pay your staff bi-weekly, then set up a repeat as bi-weekly and on your next pay date. In that instance, the data will be highly accurate and will even help you identify those months where you have three paydays instead of the usual two.

I also recommend setting the repeat date on the actual payday, rather than trying to predict exactly when the cash will exit your account in situations, such as checks clearing the bank. It's generaly best to err on the side of caution and ensure you have the cash in your account so that there's no chance of a failed payment.

It's important to set your budget up in a way that serves you, the business owner, foremost. That means it needs to be readable and organized in a way that suits you and your business. (Of course, if you are an advisor setting up the budget for your client, it means that you're setting up with their needs first, not yours. They'll love you for it.)

There are a couple common ways to structure a repeating budget. First off, if you are creating a budget manually, I recommend against using your chart of accounts as default categories for your budget. I find that, in general, those categories better serve accounting than an operational budget.

Rather, I recommend building your budget with categories and item names that are clear, organized and make the most sense for your business. Consider where you want to see your expenses on a granular level and where you many not need so much detail.

Many tools will autobuild your budget based on your accounting data. Not only is that a major time-saver, but it will help you avoid missing expenses.

Disclosure: if you don't already know, I am the co-founder of Dryrun (dryrun.com), a cash flow forecasting software for business. Although the core approach and system I am recommending in this book can be executed in a variety of ways, from a spreadsheet through to a wall and a box of crayons, my system dovetails with the approach we take in Dryrun.

However, the most important thing to me is that you are taking control of your cash flow with any tool under the sun that will help you.

In Dryrun, we pull in expenses from your cloud accounting software, analyze the data and build an automatically repeating forecast. The auto forecast may be accurate with just one click, but if not, a few quick adjustments and it's ready to go.

To be clear, the goal here isn't to build the most detailed budget humanly possible, rather, it's to break your expenses out into the fewest, meaningful categories and items for your business. The breakdown that makes it fast and easy for you to review, make changes and make predictions. Balance out the time commitment versus the granularity of the data you need to inform your decisions.

Talking with hundreds of business owners over the years as they share and discuss their recurring budget with me to better understand best practices, I've seen budgets of just a handful of items covering a large range of expenses, through to budgets built on hundreds of detailed items. One approach isn't necessarily better than the other; it comes down to which approach fits which business better and ensuring that the approach covers their needs.

The business owners usually have a good idea of which areas concern them the most, based on their intuition. Don't dwell on the details too, long – just get started. You can adjust on the fly later.

One more important factor. We're building this repeating budget based on your usual, regular expenses (and possibly income in some cases.) We'll deal with the 'one-time' or irregular expenses a bit later. We just want to start with items that repeat monthly, weekly, bi-weekly…etc. and are of a similar value every time they repeat.

If you're planning on building your budget manually (which may be the case if you don't have access to your accounting data), then you're likely staring at a blank screen, trying to figure out where to start. Ask yourself, "what is our biggest expense every month" that tends to be consistent in payment date and amount. eg. Payroll. That's often a good place to start. Grab an average amount, such as your payroll per month over the last six months, and get started.

Step one. Make a category and call it 'Payroll'. Now add your first item in the category. I recommend entering your name and your payment. Reminding yourself that you're being paid for doing such a difficult and often stressful job is a nice place to start.

IF you are a start up company and you aren't paying yourself quite yet, that's ok. Enter your name anyway and $0.00. That will set a goal in place and remind you that your top priority is to make sure you are benefiting from your endeavor.

Building your budget from there, really doesn't take a long time. Start by reviewing your credit card statement and bank statement for regular, repeating expenses. Unless you are paying cash, those records will likely contain a lot of the information you need. Leave the big, one-time bills out. We'll deal with those later

Next, dig through your receipts for items not reflected in your statements and build out a budget that covers all of your regular, core expenses.

You will also likely find expenses on your credit card or even in your bank statement that don't necessarily repeat regularly, but also aren't big bills you want to track separately. A useful tactic is to take the average of these additional expenses and enter an item as a budget line that deals with these expenses. Almost like a contingency fund for every month.

Budget Building Tips:

- make it readable and a resource for you

- use categories that make sense for you

- use item names that are clear to you

- set the repeat date to the most likely day the cash will exit your account

- if the repeat date varies somewhat, use an earlier date to stay on the safe side

- build it to auto-repeat to save you time later

- make sure it's ready to accept changes

- put in everything that repeats and are regular expenses

- leave 'one time' or irregular expenses for tracking later

- separate out bills that need to be paid later, ie. supplier bills, inventory bills, rent, taxes

- it won't be penny perfect, let alone dollar perfect

- don't get hung up with the 'exceptions', deal with them later

- syncing with cloud-accounting software may make this process painless

Fig 7. Recurring Budget

Cash Flow Actuals

JANUARY	2019	FEBRUARY	2019	MARCH	2019	APR
Month Start	$383,676	Month Start	$283,459	Month Start	$176,242	Mon
Recurring	-$100,217	Recurring	-$107,217	Recurring	-$111,717	Recu

IT/COMMUNICATIONS

Item	JANUARY	FEBRUARY	MARCH
VOIP Toll Free Number	-$55	-$55	-$55
Test Server	-$560	-$560	-$560
Video Conferencing	-$25	-$25	-$25
Online Chat Service	-$130	-$130	-$130
Email Host	-$60	-$60	-$60
Web Host	-$250	-$250	-$250
Office Phone	-$490	-$490	-$490
Mobile Phones	-$734	-$734	-$734
Total	**-$2,304**	**-$2,304**	**-$2,304**

UTILITIES

Item	JANUARY	FEBRUARY	MARCH
Power	-$225	-$225	-$225
Water/Sewage	-$165	-$165	-$165
Gas	-$225	-$225	-$225
Total	**-$615**	**-$615**	**-$615**

PAYROLL

Item	JANUARY	FEBRUARY	MARCH
Owner	-$8,400	-$8,400	-$8,400
Manager	-$5,400	-$5,400	-$5,400
Developer	-$5,600	-$5,600	-$5,600
Lead Developer	-$6,600	-$6,600	-$6,600
Creative Director	-$5,500	-$5,500	-$5,500
Designer	-$4,500	-$4,500	-$4,500
Project Manager	-$4,600	-$4,600	-$4,600
Sales	-$4,400	-$4,400	-$4,400
Technical Director	-$5,800	-$5,800	-$5,800
Office Manager	-$2,400	-$2,400	-$2,400
Jr. Designer	-$3,520	-$3,520	-$3,520
Marketing Manager	-$5,400	-$5,400	-$5,400
Marketing Assistant	-$2,900	-$2,900	-$2,900
Total	**-$65,020**	**-$65,020**	**-$65,020**

OFFICE

Item	JANUARY	FEBRUARY	MARCH
Accounting	-$2,100	-$2,100	-$2,100

Note: This recurring budget image is from a Dryrun forecast (dryrun.com) but something similar can be built in other tools, such as a spreadsheet.

Timing is Everything:
Inflows and Outflows of Cash

Now that we have the usual, repeating items in your recurring budget, it's time to turn our attention to the items that often cause shortfalls, angst and sleepless nights. The big bills that are often unexpected. Will you have enough money to pay your staff, pay your rent, pay those bills!?

So often, this is simply a case of timing. Will money come in before you need it on hand to send it back out the door? When your income is relatively consistent, such as subscription revenue, it can be a little easier to predict when money will roll in but it's nonetheless, critical to keep careful watch on your cash flow.

When you send out invoices to charge for your goods or services, things get exponentially more complicated. Predicting when you'll have money on hand gets much more complicated and shortfalls much more likely. A well-managed cash flow management system is simply required if you are to survive and thrive.

In fact, through our many conversations with businesses, it's rapidly became apparent that late payment of invoices is simply the number one issue causing cash flow shortfalls. In the end, the actual shortfall is often the result of timing issues and poor tracking.

Early in this book I introduced the problems that the timing of payments pose to a business and how poor tracking exacerbates the issue.

Let's take a short case study of how the timing of payments can cause a business serious grief:

'Janice' owns a design shop. It's Monday morning and she is looking over her week. She has a video shoot scheduled for Friday and her videographer requires an up-front payment for $7,000. Friday is also payday. She needs around $27,000 to make payroll so, in total, she needs $34,000 on hand. She logs into her bank to check her account and only has $11,000 available. She's $23,000 short.

She looks through her invoices and finds that she's expecting two payments this week from clients. The first is due on Wednesday, for $17,000. The second was due last week so she's sure it should arrive at any time. That invoice amount is for $20,000. She should have plenty to cover everything.

By Wednesday, nothing has arrived and she's getting nervous. She hops on the phone and calls both clients. Barry, promises the $20,000 check was sent last Friday so it should be in hand by the end of the day. She's going to have to trust him on that. Her other client, Sarah, says that the payment is overdue because she's waiting on payment from her customer. With a little bit of convincing, she agrees to pay $5,000 today via e-payment.

If both payments arrive as promised, she'll have $36,000 on hand. Just enough to cover everything.

Janice does the lonely walk to the mailbox, hoping the money has arrived. What a relief! The check is there and Janice rushes to the bank before it closes to get it deposited. Everything is working out... until the teller completes the deposit and hands Janice her receipt with the balance. She only has $28,000 in her account.

How could that be? She should be in the clear! Janice logs into her account back at the office and discovers that a payroll tax bill she had scheduled for payment has been withdrawn from her account. She completely forgot about it!

As frustrating as it is, Janice is fortunate that the shortfall is small enough that she can cover the amount personally and stay afloat for another week.

Shortfalls may not happen every week for businesses, but they are much too frequent. In fact, in most businesses, the number of payments coming in and going out are many times the few payments Janice experienced. Cash flow is complicated and the timing of payments pose a massive problem. From checks, through to e-payments, auto debits and credits, transfers and the like, it's a wonder businesses make it through a single month.

Too many business owners experience this sort of complication on a weekly basis. Juggling funds, making promises and flying by the seat-of-their-pants. Having just enough padding in the bank to stay afloat.

The tragic part is that too many business owners think that this sort of circumstance is simply a foregone conclusion.

It's not. Had Janice been tracking her cash flow (or better yet, hired a pro to stay on top of things), she would likely have seen the potential issue a couple of weeks out. That additional time would have offered many more alternatives to using her personal funds to stay afloat.

Banks are more likely to offer short-term relief when they see a plan in place and a lot of lead-time. Janice may also be able to move some deadlines around and receive payments earlier. She may have put off an equipment purchase that wasn't desperate and been right on top of her invoicing and payments.

You have options. That's what cash flow forecasting will do for you. Give you options and allow you to be proactive. It's no guarantee of success but your chances go up immensely.

You may have wondered why I recommend separating out the large bills, due for payemnt later, from our regular expenses. The reason is simple; it's easier to spot the bills that you still need to pay when it's isolated from that long list of small, regular expenses.

It's also easier for us to pick out the timing issues between large bill payments you need to make versus the invoice payments you are expecting to land in your account.

Depending on your business model, you may not have the 'worst case scenario' of juggling the timing of bills and invoices, alongside a host of regular expenses. Many businesses have fewer large, irregular bills, alongside income that is regular and steady. But dealing with large, irregular bills is complicated enough to warrant consistent forecasting.

Tracking Your Bills

Let's start with your bills, since you've already created a repeating budget that is likely heavy on expenses. I'm sure you've noticed that not every single expense or bill falls neatly into either your repeating budget or your bill tracking. That's completely fine. Just make a quick judgment call and track them where they make the most sense to you.

The key to tracking your bills effectively is in careful tracking of the payment dates. Make sure you are entering the bills into your forecast on the date that you expect the cash to leave your account, likely the due date. But pay close attention. Some due dates may inadvertently fall on a weekend and require payment on the last business day prior. It should be easy to spot these issues if you are entering your items via a calendar interface.

When you are creating your forecast, don't just enter the bills that are on your desk. If you are expecting bills to arrive later, enter it into your forecast right away, even if the amount and due date is an estimate. For instance, if you pay a quarterly tax bill, rough in the date and amount well ahead of time. Even set a repeating, quarterly item for a rough amount that repeats into the future indefinitely. Just having a reminder that a large payment is looming can help you make better decisions.

Of course, when the bill does arrive, you can update the entry with the actual amount and date. There is one other major benefit of roughing in the expected bill ahead of time - if the bill fails to arrive or is lost in junk mail, you will not be surprised and can follow up. Unfortunately, creditors are rarely patient when a mix-up happens and the results can be painful if you are unprepared.

Invoices

I'm covering invoices last in this chapter; however that doesn't match with their importance. Often the greatest issue that cash-starved businesses face comes down to simply getting paid on time... or even close to the due date!

In many industries and sectors, late payment of invoices is a chronic and devastating problem. We talk to business owners everyday, around the entire world. It's truly a global problem. Sending out invoices and having customers promise to pay in 30 days, 60 days, 90 days, even 120 days is difficult enough. The fact is that payments are chronically arriving months late, and at times, failing to arrive at all.

When keeping track of your invoices, it is essential to enter those items and the date that you are ***most likely to receive payment***. That is typically the due date, certainly not the invoice date. But, that is just a starting point. If you have a client that typically pays 20 days late, adjust the dates of those invoices to twenty days beyond the due date.

Then stay on top of those invoices. The second a payment is late, reach out to your customer and request that payment (very politely!) Show that you are on top of things and are serious about the prompt payment. For some clients, that is all it will take to get things back on track.

Additionally, those conversations will help you predict when the payments will actually arrive if they do not appear to be imminent. Try to get a true gauge from your client and adjust your forecast accordingly.

Non-invoiced Payments

Now I know that not all businesses send out invoices that are paid later as their main source of income. In fact, my own business is a subscription business paid via credit card on a monthly or annual basis. The reason we tackle the invoice/payment process first is that it's potentially much more volatile and dangerous from a cash flow perspective.

Many businesses are paid upon delivery of the product or service in cash, via credit card, electronic payments etc. These payments are often smaller in amount and more frequent. From a cash flow perspective, frequent, regular payments can lower your risk of a sudden and dramatic cash flow shortfall, however, cash flow issues still plague these businesses.

In these cases, tracking your revenue is just as important as keeping track of individual invoices but the way you approach your forecasts will be a little different. With numerous, smaller purchases, there is little value to tracking every single sale in your forecasts. In fact, it's likely a bad idea to attempt to track each deal as you'll end up with information overload and really no benefit.

I suggest breaking the payments up into manageable chunks, such as entering either daily or weekly sales totals into your forecast, depending on what frequency works best for you versus the additional time involved to record more granular data. Personally, I simply pull bank deposits into Dryrun from my accounting tool and auto forecast going forward, then I build out 'what if' scenarios to evaluate different growth outcomes.

You may want to break down those sales figures a little further into product lines, or service categories if that's a better fit in your circumstance. The key is to balance out the time and attention needed to enter a higher level of detail versus the usefulness of that additional information.

I always suggest leaning towards the simpler set of require-ments aiming for 'just enough' data and an adequate level of accuracy to help you make decisions. Your forecast will never be perfect, any more than a weather forecast several days out. To attempt perfection is a fool's game. But rest assured, even reasonably accurate data will be game-changing.

Averting a Crisis and Reducing Risk

Once you've built a forecast that includes your recurring budget as well as the 'one-time' or more troublesome bills and invoices, it's time to put your forecast to good use.

The major benefit of getting started today is that your forecast will significantly reduce the chances of a crisis by buying you time to take action and deal with a potential issue. Of course, your first forecast might reveal that you are facing some major issues right now! In fact, we've seen that happen many times. The very first time a business builds a forecast they discover they are right in the middle of a crisis and go into panic mode!

Business owners that dive into a forecast are often spurred to action because they see a crisis on the horizon, but at times, I suspect they unconsciously know that things aren't adding up and that leads them to wade through their cash flow bringing clarity to their intuition.

I know that fear can be a powerful motivator, but too often in the case of cash flow, it does the opposite and paralyzes people. Trust me, knowing is always better. Even if you have that uncomfortable feeling…ESPECIALLY if you have that uncomfortable feeling that something's not right in your cash flow, I encourage you to dive in and see where you're at TODAY!

If a shortfall is looming, any precious time you can give yourself to take action will improve your chances of finding a solution. Letting it run its course may keep you in 'bliss' for a short time longer but could eliminate any options you may have had for crisis aversion.

Now I hope for most of you that diving into your forecasts today shows smooth sailing ahead and highlights potential issues with tons of time and a litany of options to deal with any potential issues.

So let's take a look at setting up a process that will be efficient while serving as an early warning system.

The absolute, number one, ultimate secret to predicting and dealing with crisis?! Consistency!!! Yeah, that doesn't sound very exciting but we're really trying to reduce the 'excitement' that comes along with a potentially fatal crisis. Over the long term, consistent cash flow forecasting can significantly reduce your business risk. Little effort, high reward.

In order for your early warning system to be working, you need to check in regularly and often. You can't afford a break. Picture a lighthouse along the coast. It's reassuring light flashing several times a minute out into the night. There's a good chance, even in a dense fog, a ship's captain will see the signal with time to avoid the rocks. Now imagine that light flashing once every five minutes. It's getting a little tricky to see. Hopefully, the captain is looking towards the coast at just the right time. Now imagine the light flashing once every half hour. If it's a cloudless night then it may be seen, but any fog or inattention and the ship is running aground. Now imagine the light flashing once a week. The chances of missing the rocks comes down to a lucky break.

We see this in businesses all of the time. They've been on a lucky streak and believe it's going to continue. I suppose there's only a 30% chance that it won't continue, but I don't like those odds. Especially when turning the odds massively in your favor is a pretty simple thing to do.

So, looking at your business, how often do you need to review your cash flow to be assured you'll see the flashing light before you run aground? Daily? Weekly? Twice a month? Monthly? Honestly, I'm not going past monthly because, in business terms, monthly cash flow forecasts are more akin to the lighthouse beam flashing once every couple of hours. If it's a clear night and you're paying attention, you might get through ok.

When I hear of businesses that don't forecast their cash flow *at all*, I'm simply amazed…and disturbed. They're truly driving in the dark believing that the fact they haven't totaled their car yet is a clear indication that driving blind is foolproof. Maybe even worse, when I hear of business owners looking at cash flow statements revealing *what's already happened* somehow safeguards them moving forward, I just shake my head.

Picture driving down the highway, with your eyes closed for five minutes, then peeking in the rear-view mirror to assure yourself that you're not headed for a collision. You're looking the wrong way!

So, back to consistency. What is the right frequency for updating and reviewing your forecasts? Before you decide, let's dig into things a little deeper.

First, let's talk about ROI. Your return on investment for your time and attention. If you run out of cash, your business could die. I may be starting with the extreme case, but the numbers tell us that's not an edge case. Businesses die at a statistically tragic rate. Business death isn't just about closing your doors. It's about lost personal savings. Possibly personal bankruptcy. It will affect your spouse, partner, family. It'd just be embarrassing. So, let's try not to die. That alone should be worth a half hour a week, shouldn't it?

Let's look at the other risks you run. A cash flow shortfall can stunt your businesses growth. The money you need to have on hand could cause you to miss out on a deal because you can't fund the materials, the expansion, the contractors…any number of things.

Shortfalls take up an incredible amount of time and attention. Even if, in the end, you line up the funds necessary to fight another day, you waste so much time dealing with everything. Meeting with bankers, investors, clients, suppliers and pleading your case at every turn. You don't get that time back and it's guaranteed to hit at the worst possible moment. If avoiding a crisis outright isn't in the cards, I'm sure you'd agree that dealing with the issues on your own terms and time line is much better than being backed into a corner and working on everyone else's clock.

Cash flow issues aren't just about shortfalls. You may very well have money in the bank but imagine getting funds rolling in that build up your savings and could fund your growth? Extra money on hand fuels that growth. It helps you in your business development, marketing and expansion.

Finally, the more frequently you update and review your forecasts, the less time it takes for each session. When things are up to date, your check-ins can be very quick yet highly effective. When everything's left for too long, just getting started takes a lot of time and attention. Figuring out where you left off, where everything is at, digging up documents and dealing with long forgotten details is painful.

Is that enough pain for you? We haven't even delved into the benefits of setting and tracking sales goals and planning for growth, that'll come later. Right now, we're focused completely on crisis aversion.

I'll point out here that you've spent more time reading just this single chapter then you'd likely have to spend on your cash flow every week if you stay consistent. Your business can be revolutionized over your Monday cup of coffee if you spend it updating your forecasts.

Another sneak preview here: imagine handing off those duties to an accounting pro that keeps an eye on everything. Your duties were just reduced, allowing you to spend even more time on growing your business all the while having someone watch your back. You can have your cake and eat it too! We'll explore that recommendation in a later chapter.

I'm hoping that you have agreed to a regular check-in on your cash flow. Weekly is a good place to start for most businesses but I'll leave that decision up to you. Next, let's look at a simple process for staying on top of your near term cash flow.

Cash Flow Management Process

I'm going to outline a process that I suggest is a good starting point for regular cash flow forecasting in terms of dealing with your near term cash flow and crisis prevention.

1. Book it

Put a time in your calendar and set up reminders so that you are checking in on a regular, consistent basis. I suggest early in the week to give yourself time to take action on a few key items. So, let's say Monday at 10:30 am for arguments sake.

2. Update Your Bookkeeping

You need your bookkeeping up-to-date. I highly recommend using an accounting pro that can keep you right up-to-date, so when you sit down to review your forecasts, the basic info is current. Today, this is often more about reconciling your data then old school data entry. You're up-to-date on your expenses, you know what bills are due and when, and you know who owes you money and when it's due to come in.

3. Highlight Overdue Items

Anything that's overdue is a cause for concern. Do you have outstanding invoices that your clients have failed to pay on time? Are there any bills that you've neglected to pay and which are now in arrears? In many cases, these overdue items are the cause of critical shortfalls. Start here.

4. Predict When the Overdue Items Will Clear

Here's the key. Predict when those items will realistically be paid and update your forecast accordingly. Once an item is overdue, tracking items by their due dates is dangerous.

If someone owes you money and it's overdue, you need to deal with it *right now*! This is the first item on your action list. Pick up the phone and find out when that payment is likely to arrive. There's much more to dealing with late payments that we will explore later but for our purposes right now, let's focus on updating your forecast to make it as accurate as possible.

Similarly, if you are overdue on a bill you need to pay, be sure to follow up. Your creditor may be more flexible and understanding with regular, consistent updates and a plan to pay off what you owe.

5. Look for Potential Shortfalls

Now that your forecast is updated, you need to look for potential issues and shortfalls. You should be able to identify when you'll dip into the red. If you've been forecasting regularly, nothing should be that big of a surprise, but your understanding of your situation, the gravity and potential outcomes should be clear.

Build out 'what if' scenarios to evaluate your options and develop a plan.

6. Take Action When Required

If you're headed for crisis, start the process of dealing with the issue immediately. Don't ignore the problem. Get on it today!

That's a basic work-flow and process for your regular cash flow check-ins. Consistency is key. If your check-ins are short, positive and 'boring' every week, then celebrate. That's a good thing. But keep it up as long as your business is alive and breathing. It's the key to averting crisis and the investment in time is minuscule compared to the benefit you receive.

We'll look at the details of setting up a 'cloud-based' system that will help you revolutionize your business, streamline and automate tasks and help you take control of your cash flow. Before we dive into the specifics, we need to look at the longer term and make sure you can reach your goals and grow your business.

Part 3

Revenue Forecasts and Growth Planning

Setting and Making Your Revenue Goals

Up to this point, we have been focused on dealing with your
near term cash flow. The money is expected to flow in and
flow out in the next few days and weeks. Often timing issues
are the direct culprit in a shortfall. Setting up and managing a
system to deal with your near term 'actuals' forecast is essential, but shortfalls aren't always a result of timing issues and
late payments.

If you have a shortfall today, there's a good chance that you
have a sales issue going back months in time and are simply
not bringing enough money into the business overall. In other
words, if you need to make one million this year to cover your
costs and retain a profit, you need to figure out how you are
going to make that money and get it coming in within your
twelve month time line.

Setting a revenue goal is essential for running a healthy
business and maintaining cash flow. In fact, outside of late

payments, one of the greatest stresses on cash flow is simply too little revenue from a shortfall in sales. How do you know if you're generating enough sales to cover your costs, generate a profit and grow your business?

The first step is to gain an understanding of the amount of money you need to earn to stay in business every month. We can take a step back and look at your monthly recurring budget to get a very basic 'break-even' point. Simply multiplying your monthly budget by twelve can serve as a starting point to predicting your revenue needs for the year.

So, let's say that your regular repeating expenses in your budget are $100,000 every month. Then can we say that your revenue goal for the year is $1.2 million? Well, that's a very basic starting point but unlikely to serve our needs. Let's look a little closer.

What other costs will you incur over the year? What costs are not included in your regular budget but are required to generate your product or service? We will refer to these additional costs as your cost of goods sold or COGS for short. These costs are directly related to a sale. For instance, if you manufacture a product, the raw materials would be a key part of your COGS.

Let's say that your directly related costs for generating $100,000 in goods and services is $50,000, then you would need to sell $200,000 worth of goods in a month just to cover your $100,000 in expenses plus the $100,000 in COGS to simply break even.

Of course, you also need to earn a profit in order to create value in your company, pay out shareholders (such as yourself) and to grow your business. If you want to generate a 10% profit margin, you will need to generate $220,000 in revenue every month.

But business is never quite that smooth. You need to build an emergency fund to deal with the inevitable, unexpected costs that will certainly come your way. Let's say you want to generate an additional $10,000 every month to build the contingency funds. Now you need monthly sales in excess of $230,000 per month.

Even this basic example is getting quite complicated. You can see that the business in this example needs to set a goal of $230,000 a month or $2,760,000 per year in order to sustainably grow their business.

Now you have a goal in mind for your annual revenue as well as your monthly revenue. Here's where the rubber meets the road. You need a sales process tied with consistent and detailed tracking in order to prioritize and reach your goals.

From Goals to Sales

Now that you have your goal, you need to figure out how to execute and generate that revenue but a lot of questions come to mind:

How will you get those jobs coming in? When will they come in? What if they all come in at the same time? Will you run into capacity issues and need to pay overtime and contractors? Could you miss your deadlines?

Understanding your sales goals and building a plan to execute is critical but timing is everything. Knowing when your business needs to deliver and when the cash will come in is essential for success.

Sales forecasts are so critical that I'm going to walk you through some basic concepts and processes to help you get started.

A Big Deal Can Mean Big Complications

Since big deals generally lead to big invoices and often, big bills, they can be the leading cause of cash flow issues. Therefore, we're going to spend some serious time exploring a typical sales process. Project-based businesses and manufacturers are just a couple of the business types that are often at the mercy of closing big deals.

If you're business is reliant on consistent, small sales feel free to jump ahead if you want to stick to the details of your business, but I think you'll find this next section useful to know.

When you're business is dependent on landing larger deals, your sales pipeline can often feel highly unpredictable, feast or famine and out of control. Too often business owners believe that as long as they are landing enough deals to stay ahead of their expenses, they are doing all they can. Trust me, bringing some structure and sophistication to your sales process will help you avoid a crisis, reach your goals and grow your business.

Simply put, you need an accurate, consistently updated and reviewed sales forecast to maintain healthy cash flow and grow. (Alternatively "revenue" - if that term is more comfortable for you.) A sales forecast will help you prioritize tasks, make critical decisions and time your growth. Too often businesses view a sales forecast as nothing more than a list of potential deals. That's not a forecast that can drive your growth, that's just a dream.

Two key issues prevent a sales forecast from having a level of accuracy that makes it highly usable for a business to make critical decisions. First, it's the timing of the deals. I've seen this problem numerous times and have been guilty of it in the past as well, until the problem hit us first hand. When a sales forecast consists of a list of potential deals, with no prediction of when the deal may close and you will have to deliver your product or service, you're running in the dark. Second, how likely are you to close the deals and turn them into money?

Deal Timing

First, let's look at the timing of the deals. For example, let's say you look at a list of deals and your best guess is that the deals you're attempting to close total $2 million. If you need to generate $1 million to break even this year, then all is good right? One key factor is when these deals will potentially close.

If they take two years to close and turn into money, you'll likely be short of cash. If they all close next month, you may be overwhelmed and unable to deliver everything on time. Do you have the inventory on hand or the staffing required to offer your services in such a short window of time?

Of course, that example is simplified and extreme. It does illustrate the issue of timing. If it takes too long for deals to close you simply won't have enough revenue turning into cash flow. Alternatively, if the deals close in bunches, you might not have the staff or resources to deliver as promised and short term relief, such as paying overtime or hiring contractors quickly eats up your profit margin and can even cause you to lose money on deals.

Too often business owners fly by the seat of their pants. They run on instinct and hope for a big dose of luck to make it through the month and the year. It's simply not a recipe for success. I've seen it so many times before. A sales forecast that is nothing more than a list of 'potentials' in a spreadsheet.

I remember when I was at the same stage. In my last business, a creative agency, I was scanning down a list of deals we were in various stages of discussing. Some were little more than rumors of projects that still only had a rough budget attached. Others were in the final stages of negotiation. I remember looking at the tally at the bottom of the page. It was over $1 million in deals. Ok, great. However, what does that mean? I figured we should land around 70% of the deals, so, we could land over $700K in total.

Then the realization hit me. What if all these deals landed at the same time? A cold shiver ran down my spine. If they all landed at once, we wouldn't be able to deliver with the resources we had and we simply couldn't expand fast enough to deal with all of that work. That's when I significantly upgraded my sales forecast to include the likely timing of those deals. Although it was a very rudimentary sales forecast, it was a significant step up in sophistication.

It allowed me to see clearly where the peaks and valleys were likely to be. When we needed to ramp up our sales and negotiate timelines to keep us busy and when we needed to pull back or turn away work to fit our capacity. It gave me a much better idea of how and when to grow our team.

It is critical that you look at these deals **on a time line** to predict when they will most likely close and turn into cash flow. This time line will help you understand if you have enough deals in your pipeline as well as if there are serious peaks or valleys in your sales that will lead to staff sitting idle or a lack of capacity to deliver.

Deal Probability

Of course, you're unlikely to close all of the deals. The second part of the equation that is critical to understand is how likely are you to close a sale and turn it into cash. If you have a number of deals (hopefully, now viewed on a time line) of $2 million, how many of those deals are you likely to close? In other words, what is the probability you will win the deal?

Deal probability is a process of predicting how likely you will win a deal, based on the stage of the sales process that a deal sits. This process can help bring some historical and realistic data into the equation, beyond your 'gut feeling'. We'll take a closer look at this tactic in the next chapter.

Building a Realistic Forecast
with Deal Probability

Deal probability brings a dose of reality to your sales forecasts. Weighting your potential deals gives you a more sophisticated data set that is standardized and more likely to be usable for management decisions.

Deal probability, also known as "deal weighting," is the process of assigning a percentage to the likelihood that a deal will successfully close based on stage of the sales pipeline where it currently sits. If you've been in business for some time, you will likely have a decent grasp on your typical sales process. If not, that's ok, we'll help you come up with a basic set of stages that you can use as a starting point and evolve into a set of stages that better matches your actual sales process as you gain experience with your clients and sales process.

Let's take a look at an example of a sales pipeline and then we'll explore how we can apply deal weighting to the stages to get a better grasp on our potential revenue.

For example, let's say you have a six-stage sales pipeline.

Stage 1: Lead is identified

In this example, identifying a lead means a prospect has reached out to you or that you've picked out a potential customer to contact and see if they have a need for your product or service. Generating leads that are likely to be a bona fide prospect is important so that you aren't wasting your time talking to the wrong people.

How do you generate leads? From referral? From advertising? Networking? Cold-Calling?

One of the most useful things you can do is keep careful track of which lead generating channels are providing the most prospects that work their way through the process to a sale. That will help you spend money and resources in the right place.

Stage 2: Qualifying a Lead via a Discovery Call

It's important not to waste either your time or the leads time if they really aren't a fit for your business and unlikely to buy. A short call can help you identify those leads that are 'qualified' to move to the next step in your sales process and set up those next steps.

In this example, the qualified lead will be taken through a demonstration of your product so create a concrete next step and book a time for the demo.

Stage 3: Product demo

I could go on for pages about this step. I hate even calling it a demo. This stage is more about discussing the benefits of your product to their business and dealing with potential objections ahead of time. But, staying on topic, we'll use a product demo as an example stage.

Stage 4: Proposal Provided

Once they've agreed that you are offering a solution that will benefit their business they are ready to take the next step and look at a formal outline of your product or service, the time line for delivery, and the price.

Stage 5: In Negotiation

Often there will be some negotiation before a contract is signed, sealed and delivered.

Stage 6: Deal is Closed (Won or lost.)

When a deal is won, a contract is signed and the deal moves onto delivery and payment.

Ok, so there's an example of a sales pipeline and process. What are the stages of your sales process? What makes the most sense for your clients? What critical stages are they likely to go through in order to get to a finalized deal?

Once you have your stages outlined, you can dig into the likelihood that a deal will be won, based on the stage of the sales process where it sits. If you have the data on hand based on historic sales, terrific, but I suspect that many of you don't have those numbers available. That's ok. We're going to start at the beginning and apply some guesstimate numbers as a starting point. Over time, you will be able to refine these numbers based on the data you will gather with your sales forecasts.

Applying Deal Probability

Now we can apply 'weighting' to each stage of our sales pipeline in order to better predict the likely revenue we will gain through our sales.

Here's a basic example of applying deal probability to a sales pipeline.

Let's say your typical deal is $100,000; you could assign a potential deal value of $100,000 to every lead in every stage of your pipeline. The issue, of course, is that you are very unlikely to win every deal. (If you are winning nearly all of your deals, you may be pricing your product or service too low.)

We don't want to assign every lead a value of $100,000 when, in the end, just a few of those leads will make it all the way through to become a completed deal.

In order to create more accurate sales forecasts, it is useful to assign a probability weighting to each stage of the pipeline in order to bring some sense of reality to the figures.

First, let's look at a basic list of deals.

20 deals x $100,000 = $2 million in sales

Really, not very useful. There's no indication of which of those deals are likely to close and which are likely to be lost.

Let's look at our sales pipeline above. If we had 20 deals in various stages of the pipeline, each valued at $100,000, there is still potential revenue of $2,000,000.

1) Lead is identified: 7 deals valued at $700,000

2) Qualified via discovery call: 4 deals at $400,000

3) Product demo: 3 deals at $300,000

4) Proposal provided: 2 deals at $200,000

5) In negotiation: 1 deal at $100,000

6) Deal is won: 3 deals at $300,000

Total: $2,000,000

A closer look at this pipeline will reveal that over one third of the deals (those in stage one) are leads that haven't even been contacted yet to be qualified as a bonafide prospect. Let's say that only one out of ten of those leads are even qualified on average, it is completely misleading to have them each valued at $100,000. In fact, until a prospect has been contacted and qualified, there's likely too little information to even assign a value or predict the chance of closing those deals until you have a good set of data over time to take into account.

The next stage currently contains deals worth an assigned value of $400,000. Although the initial call went well with the lead and they are interested in learning more about your product, the likelihood of closing a deal after this initial call is still low, but assigning a likelihood of closing a deal at this point is reasonable.

How accurate will the prediction be? That really depends on a few factors, such as the number of deals your business has closed in the past and how well you've tracked that data to be used in your forecast. The more you've closed and the more accurately the deal stages have been tracked, the more accurate your probability weighting will be.

Calculating Probability

Calculating probability is as simple as assigning a percentage to the deals in a stage. For instance, let's say that you tend to close around 10% of the qualified prospects in stage two of your pipeline and you have $400,000 of potential deals in that stage, then your weighted deals would be worth $40,000 not $400,000.

Similarly, we can assign percentages to each stage of the pipeline and we will see a much different picture emerge:

Stage 1: Lead is identified
7 deals valued at $700,000 x 1% probability = $7,000

Stage 2: Qualified via Discovery Call
4 deals at $400,000 x 10% probability = $40,000

Stage 3: Product Demo
3 deals at $300,000 x 30% probability = $90,000

Stage 4: Proposal Provided
2 deals at $200,000 x 50% probability = $100,000

Stage 5: In negotiation
1 deal at $100,000 x 90% probability of closing = $90,000

Stage 6: Deal is Won
3 deals at 100% = $300,000

Total: **$627,000** of $2,000,000 in potential deals

Now the numbers reflect a weighted revenue and are more realistic. Instead of predicting $2,000,000 in sales, the weighted value shows expected revenue of $627,000 – less than a third of total deals.

The Benefits of Using Deal Probability

The process of assigning deal probability to 'weight' a stage in the sales process can provide a much clearer picture of the actual sales/revenue likely to be gained from a set of deals.

Since it is critical for businesses to have an accurate and realistic forecast of their revenue, deal weighting can help both sales managers and management more accurately assess their progress versus their sales goals.

On a micro level, the data can provide a set of metrics that may help evaluate individual sales staff. It can be useful to see how different sales staff close at specific stages of the sales pipeline compared to historic closing rates. This data can help you assess training needs and opportunities to refine your overall pipeline.

For management/ownership, weighted sales forecasts can provide a crisper assessment of where sales are expected to go versus the businesses revenue goals. That can help management diagnose problems such as potential capacity or cash flow issues ahead of time, giving them time to plan proactively.

Weaknesses in Deal Probability

There has been some criticism of using deal probability in a sales forecast due to its inherent inaccuracy. It is a forecast after all. Simply put, using deal probability is significantly more accurate than tracking the total value of deals and assigning weight to stages is both efficient and relatively accurate versus the alternatives.

One suggested alternative to assigning general probability to stages is to evaluate individual deals. In this approach, sales staff are tasked with making judgment calls on the likelihood that an individual deal will close.

Although this approach may provide more accuracy, (my personal opinion is that it is unlikely) it has several key issues that plague this approach.

First, even if the approach was proven more accurate, the lack of a reliable and automated reporting process means that the data is not nearly as accessible. In other words, if (or should I say "when") sales staff fail to update deal probability in their forecasts as soon as a deal appears to progress forward, the accuracy of the data is compromised.

In addition, there really isn't a reasonable way to manually update the probability per deal, reflect that in the value of the deal and report that up to management in a seamless, efficient and up-to-the-minute manner.

The second, more glaring issue is that evaluating individual deals brings in a big dose of confirmation bias combined with a lack of standardization in the estimation of closing rates.

Asking a salesperson, 'what are the chances this deal closes' might feel right, but the amount of experience a person has combined with their overall mood that day can lead to widely ineffective guesses versus data gleaned from a large number of past deals and documented conversion rates.

My suggestion is that deal probability can not only set a reasonably accurate projection for closing deals, but its highly efficient implementation provides easily accessible data that helps in the business decision process from the sales team all the way through to ownership.

However, in order to maintain accuracy, a constant evaluation of the closing rates, updating the stage probabilities and evaluating input from your sales team can give the best set of data with the least friction possible.

Making it Effective

So, in practical terms, how can we make deal probability more effective?

The first factor is the accuracy applied to the stages. If you haven't been tracking the closing rates or have not locked down a set of stages that meet your needs quite yet, then you will have to start with your best educated guess. Whether or not you have a significant number of deals to track, make sure that you check on the rates regularly and adjust the figures as the picture becomes more refined. The higher the volume of deals in your calculations, the more accurate your rates will be.

Recognize the numbers for what they are: a forecast. It'll never be 100% accurate so err on the side of caution when you are setting goals and judging sales performance. The larger the set of data and longer the time frame, the more accurate the correlations will likely be.

Finally, a key factor that will lead to forecasts that are more accurate is a rigorously defined set of criteria for what constitutes a stage, and the requirements to move a prospect forward in your sales process. In the end, it is still up to individual sales staff to judge what stage a prospect is at in the sales cycle.

Some stages are inherently clearer but in some cases there's much more room to differ from salesperson to salesperson. For instance, what constitutes moving a lead to a qualified prospect based on a phone call? What questions need to be answered? What criteria was met to move a lead forward?

The Power of a Timeline

In the deal probability examples we've covered, there is still a major weakness in our forecasts. They are still presented as a list! There's no indication of when a deal is likely to close, when cash will start rolling in, even which month, quarter or year that the revenue could be applied. So, we have a better understanding of the amount of sales we should generate but not when.

The key is to take your weighted deals and lay them out on a time line so that you can see both how much is likely to close but also when.

To meet your goals you need to understand them. Taking those goals and laying out the deals on a time line to compare against your monthly, quarterly and yearly goals will revolutionize your business. It will not only help you reach your goals by focusing you on what you need to do and when, it will also help you identify capacity issues and address them ahead of time.

Probability will only take you so far. We still need to deal with those timing issues. See Fig. 8, where I've included a screenshot from a sales forecast in Dryrun. You can see the deals both on a time line from month to month as well as the

Fig 8. Sales Forecast with Weighted Deals

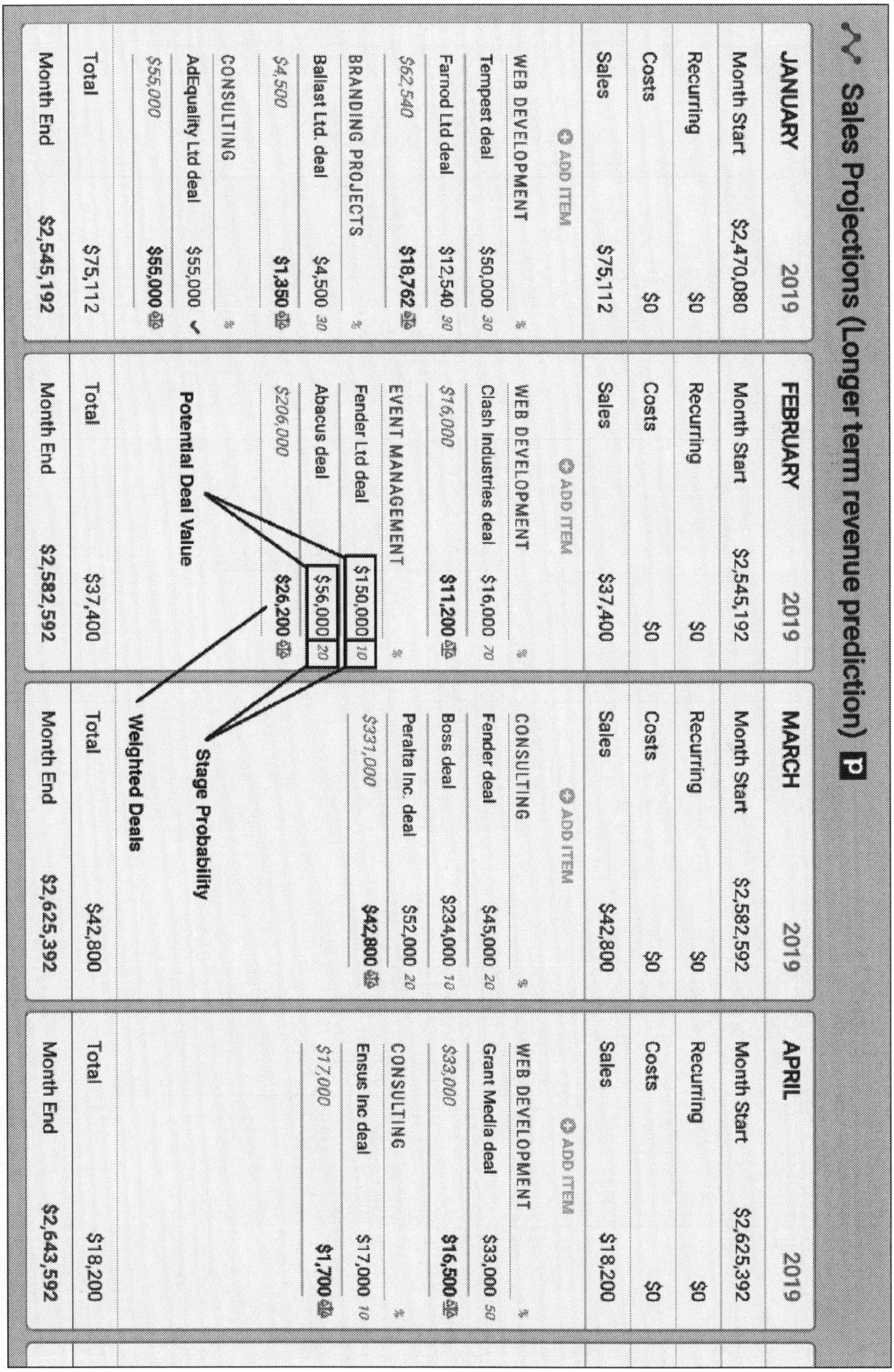

Sales Projections (Longer term revenue prediction) 🅿

Labels: Potential Deal Value · Stage Probability · Weighted Deals

JANUARY 2019

Month Start	$2,470,080	
Recurring	$0	
Costs	$0	
Sales	$75,112	

⊕ ADD ITEM

Deal	Potential Deal Value	Stage Probability (%)	Weighted
WEB DEVELOPMENT			
Tempest deal	$50,000	30	
Farnod Ltd deal	$12,540	30	
	$62,540		**$18,762**
BRANDING PROJECTS			
Ballast Ltd deal	$4,500	30	
	$4,500		**$1,350**
CONSULTING			
AdEquality Ltd deal	$55,000	✓	
	$55,000		**$55,000**

Total	$75,112
Month End	$2,545,192

FEBRUARY 2019

Month Start	$2,545,192	
Recurring	$0	
Costs	$0	
Sales	$37,400	

⊕ ADD ITEM

Deal	Potential Deal Value	Stage Probability (%)	Weighted
WEB DEVELOPMENT			
Clash Industries deal	$16,000	70	
	$16,000		**$11,200**
EVENT MANAGEMENT			
Fender Ltd deal	$150,000	10	
Abacus deal	$56,000	20	
	$206,000		**$26,200**

Total	$37,400
Month End	$2,582,592

MARCH 2019

Month Start	$2,582,592	
Recurring	$0	
Costs	$0	
Sales	$42,800	

⊕ ADD ITEM

Deal	Potential Deal Value	Stage Probability (%)	Weighted
CONSULTING			
Fender deal	$45,000	20	
Boss deal	$234,000	10	
Peralta Inc. deal	$52,000	20	
	$331,000		**$42,800**

Total	$42,800
Month End	$2,625,392

APRIL 2019

Month Start	$2,625,392	
Recurring	$0	
Costs	$0	
Sales	$18,200	

⊕ ADD ITEM

Deal	Potential Deal Value	Stage Probability (%)	Weighted
WEB DEVELOPMENT			
Grant Media deal	$33,000	50	
	$33,000		**$16,500**
CONSULTING			
Ensus Inc deal	$17,000	10	
	$17,000		**$1,700**

Total	$18,200
Month End	$2,643,592

probability that they will close. In this example, the deals have been synced with an online sales tool called Pipedrive. Using Pipedrive and Dryrun, your sales forecast is created in a click and ready for analysis. Of course, you can build these sales forecasts in other tools as well.

12

The Final Leg on the Stool: Profit

Now that we've explored revenue and established the need for consistent, detailed sales forecasts, we need to dive into the third key leg that can affect your cash flow, survival and growth. Your profit.

Simply put, profit is what's leftover after you've paid all of your expenses.

A quick refresher:

Your gross profit is your revenue minus your COGS (cost of goods sold.) But the really important figure is your net profit, your revenue minus ALL of your costs and expenses. The reason your net profit is the most important figure to track is that your business could have a high gross profit yet still lose money if your other expenses eat up any money that's left over.

I've seen business owners look at gross profit and assume all was good. In reality, they were bleeding money at the end of the day. It's easy to do. You look at a product and see a massive profit margin and think "how could we not make money with that huge profit margin?!" Gross profit margin is certainly useful to know and increasing your margins can be highly beneficial to your bottom line, but in the end, your net profit IS your bottom line. Math doesn't lie.

Profit is necessary for both business survival, growth and delivering a benefit to the business owners and investors as a reward for the significant risk they are taking. Both business owners and investors want to recoup their investment but also see some sort of additional return.

Conversely, the lack of profit will eventually mean death to your business. Without profit, your business is constantly bleeding and diving further into debt. Unfortunately, business owners too often focus nearly exclusively on revenue and cash flow yet fail to calculate accurately whether they are retaining profit.

There's a famous saying: "Revenue is vanity. Profit is sanity. Cash is reality."

It's true in so many ways. Business owners see high revenue and think that they "must be in good standing" by just bringing in plenty of revenue. But the business needs to be profitable or they are headed for closure sooner or later. Thus the 'sanity' in profit. Of course, we've seen that the number one and quickest killer of business is a lack of cash flow. That's where reality hits.

So, for your long term survival, business health and growth you must retain a profit. Not only can those extra funds be returned to the owners and investors, they can be retained in the business and used to fuel growth. Retained profits can be used to fund expansion, hire new staff, purchase equipment, accelerate marketing and sales initiatives, and of course, build up emergency funds for use in a pinch.

Profit isn't just essential for your business operations; it's also a major indication for banks, investors and other lenders that your business is a safe bet. So not only can it provide an internal safety net, it can also help you access outside funds you may require to overcome a rough patch or fuel growth.

The Golden Metric - Profit Margin

Let's take a little closer look into profit by comparing the profit margins of two fictional companies to see how important profit margins are to business stability and health.

Here's a tale of two companies in the exact same industry:

Dave's Dynamic Speaker Systems earned revenue of $1,000,000 last year. His total costs were $900,000, which means they earn a profit of $100K.

Darla's Audio Explosion earned revenue of $500,000. Her total costs were $400K, so her company earned profit of $100K as well.

Dave generated double the revenue of Darla and a tidy 10% profit margin. Darla had half the revenue but the identical profit of $100,000. The real difference is that Darla's profit margin was 20%, double that of Dave's.

Which is better? Double the revenue or double the profit margin?

Well, business changes, almost daily. The market can change, costs can go up, and sales can drop. In business, always expect the unexpected. The reality is that Dave is at a much higher risk when things inevitably change. There is little room for error. What can seem to be even a minor increase in costs can eat away at that 10% profit margin, while a greater challenge can destroy their profit and put them into the red. Darla's larger profit margin simply gives her more room to move.

Now this is a highly simplified example without diving into all of the other potential factors that will affect a business. I put it forward as an example of how your net profit margin can be a leading metric to help you understand and grow your business when it's reviewed alongside your other key metrics.

So how do you increase profit margin? Really, there are only two ways. Increase your prices or reduce your costs. Of course, that's easier said than done. Both tactics can be a significant challenge and I can't tell you which will help you most in your situation. It's likely a carefully planned and executed combination of both.

In the end, it's critical to know your gross profit, net profit, and profit margins to see the entire picture. It's also important to look at these key metrics at a much more granular level to see which of your products or services are driving the most profit for you.

I'll be honest; it's not as simple as identifying your highest profit product and focusing your business exclusively on it. (Although in some situations, it may be that simple.) It's much more likely that you have some products that are easier to sell, have a larger market opportunity and they really drive consistent revenue but may not have the highest profit margins.

While some products or services may carry the load in generating profit but it's simply not feasible to focus exclusively on them since other factors affect the overall picture.

The key is to uncover the underlying data. Conduct a thorough analysis and run different 'what if' scenarios to find a good mix that generates the revenue that you need to reach your goals while providing the profit you need for business health. All while driving the cash flow you require to survive another day.

13

Growth Planning

Now that we've covered dealing with near term cash flow, setting and reaching revenue goals, and looking at the improving profit margins, we turn our attention to growth. Business growth is both essential for health and stability but it can also be the riskiest action you will take with your business. Stable and sustainable growth requires significant planning and forecasting to ensure things go as smoothly as possible and you are prepared to deal with the inevitable difficulties that spring up.

Of course, the risk that goes along with growth, especially fast growth, is part of the challenge for a healthy business. Growing revenue and profits can fuel your expansion, create more jobs, empower you to serve more customers, and hopefully you can benefit financially as the business owner that has put so much at stake.

The risk in growth often comes from basing expansion on limited or misleading data, such as a short burst of increased business that you expect to continue with little evidence to support your assertion. Sometimes, growth is a poorly planned attempt to address systemic problems with the belief that growth will somehow fix issues that rot at the core of a business. Expansion is so often ill-timed, ill-planned and under-funded, leading to failure.

Yet timing, planning and funding are all issues that can be addressed through data, realistic forecasts and exploring potential scenarios to prepare for both expected and unexpected eventualities. It's all about truly understanding your current reality and predicting likely outcomes so that you're planning for the best and prepared for the worst. Predictable, sustainable growth that's well funded and carefully planned leads to best-case outcomes and your best chance at sustainable growth.

Let's look at growth planning in a little more detail.

Your Current and Near Term Cash Position

First, it's critical to understand where you sit at this moment before you start diving into the future. Answer yourself these questions: What is your current cash position? You can find this out from a near term 'actuals' cash flow forecast. Do you have capital on hand right now? How does your cash flow look for the next few weeks? Are there outstanding receivables that you need to collect before you undertake costly expansion? Do you owe payments on bills in the near term? Do you owe money that is already overdue? Overall, how healthy is your current financial position?

Your Growth Rate

Next, take a close look at your growth rate. How fast have you grown over the past quarter? The past year? What's your annual growth over the past several years? What has driven that growth? Are there specific products or services that have been central to your success?

Knowing what is driving your growth is critical for the next key step: truly predicting whether your growth is likely to continue and is sustainable moving forward. It's important to take a dispassionate and analytical view of the data and look at your business through a highly analytical lens. Fooling yourself here could lead to disaster. It's simply imperative that you understand the drivers of your growth in order to be highly confident that the growth will continue as you expect.

Of course, as we've already discussed, revenue is only one factor. Your business needs to be profitable for sustainable growth. It may be that growth is one of the ways that you can increase your profit margin. For this to work, ensure that your predictions are accurate and based on hard numbers rather than a belief that growth will automatically lead to efficiencies of scale and increased profit.

Revenue Projections

In order to move from an understanding of your growth to an actual forecast, it's time to build a revenue projection to explore the future. For the next few months and quarters, this forecast is essentially a sales forecast as we've covered in the previous chapter. This revenue forecast will set the foundation for the near to mid-term growth prediction so that you can better understand how much capital you will need to undertake your expansion.

How accurate have your sales forecasts been in the past? How many deals and how much potential revenue do you have in the pipeline? Are you able to rely on your projections to be reasonably on-point? How long can you run at your current capacity based on your sales projections? Are you able to continue to deliver while you grow?

As you continue to model out your expansion, it's prudent to reach out further in the future and predict whether your expansion will be sustainable and continue. That means that your forecast will move from a near to mid-term sales projection, to a much longer prediction of growth, likely reaching out years into the future. The further out you go, the less likely the forecast will be completely accurate, and nonetheless, it's an essential tool in your toolbox. I strongly caution that you create various scenarios exploring best and worst scenarios then build out, in your mind, an accurate 'likely' scenario.

Your Long Term Growth Projection and Goal

Now that you've modeled out near, mid and long-term scenarios, it's time to establish your goals. What amount of revenue will meet your goals? How much profit is required to meet your goals? How far out can you set goals with a level of certainty? What is the best case you can reasonably imagine? Now what is the worst-case scenario?

It's important to set goals that are both optimistic and challenging, yet also within the realm of realistic possibility. Your goals should be both motivating and set a line in the sand. I recommend building out numerous 'what if' scenarios to evaluate a wide range of outcomes and potential issues so that when you set your goals there is a foundation of logic and data behind your numbers.

Narrowing in on a goal and creating a forecast as a guiding tool will help you evaluate your progress and adjust your goals on the fly. You can run this forecast alongside your near-term cash flow forecast and your mid-term sales forecast to keep track of your actuals while maintaining an eye on your true growth goals. The fact is that you should expect growth to be much more expensive and complicated than you predicted and your operations will be under stress for much more than you'd ever believed possible. The long-term growth projection will likely need to be adjusted frequently to maintain some level of realism.

Cash Flow to Fuel Your Growth

Circling all the way back to the core topic of this book, it's absolutely essential that you keep a highly consistent and careful eye on your near term cash flow during your expansion. In the end, cash flow is likely still your greatest risk factor during your expansion. Now that you have a plan in place, evaluate how much cash you will need on hand. How much of a contingency fund makes sense based on your forecasts? How can you lower your risk? What happens if you run into a shortfall?

It's prudent to have more than contingency funds available. Make sure you have contingency plans as well. Can you slow your growth if a shortage of funds hits your business? Do you have an emergency budget in place that you can use to quickly steam line your operations and cut your costs? Do you have lenders in mind that may be able to help you over any rough spots?

Lean on Advisors

I'm sure by now you can see how complicated and risky expansion is likely to be. I highly recommend that you bring other opinions and viewpoints into the process. Of course, if you have business partners, that's likely an expectation. Can you bring in other trusted advisors from outside your business that can give you a more objective opinion? Someone that can ask questions that you may not have considered? Of course, an accounting professional should definitely be on your list and involved in the planning right from the beginning. Are there others that could offer some valuable advice? Do you have advisors or mentors that can give you some honest help?

The right advisor will ask you many questions to help you see the bigger picture and explore areas you may have overlooked. I would be cautious of an advisor that doesn't ask questions, does not seem to understand what your business is about and what you are planning to do, yet has a lot of advice ready to fly. When you do have the right people asking insightful questions, engaging in fruitful debates and discussions, you are in a much stronger position than attempting to tackle this monumental task on your own.

Just remember that despite all of the potential questions and opinions, in the end, the decision is up to you. Not only will you have to live with your decision; you are likely the one facing the most risk, so know where you stand and all of your options to the best of your ability before you dive into the chaos of growth.

One last thought on growth. I remember when I first started my first business back in 1999 or so. There's a quote, and I can't honestly remember where I heard it or whose quote it is, but it was essentially this: *business is all about reducing risk.* It runs counter to so many risk-related ideas about business. The fact is that business is inherently risky.

The truth is that success in business is more likely to be based on solid execution than blind faith and a can-do attitude. Entrepreneurs generally have a solid dose of both, but a drive to reduce their risk within the confines of the endeavor they are pursuing, is not only smart, but will likely increase your chances of survival and success. That's why it's useful to maintain a mindset of reducing risk. It might just be taking that risk that's 95/100 and bringing it down to 85/100 but it could be the action that saves your business and sets you up for success.

Part 4

Establishing the System and Processes in Your Business

14

Moving to a Highly Efficient and Collaborative System

It's Time to Leave Spreadsheets Behind

Now let's focus on building a workable solution for long-term financial health. The will to manage your business better is generally present in an entrepreneur, but prioritization and attention wanes when the task proves to be highly time-consuming and frustrating. In order to consistently manage your cash flow, it's important to set up processes and a system that is clear, efficient and simple.

Let's start with the system itself. Over and over, I've seen businesses using a basic spreadsheet to manage their cash flow (if at all). In fact, as I mentioned at the beginning of this book, that's exactly where I started as well. As flexible and simple as a spreadsheet is to use for just such a purpose, it begins to show its flaws early on as minor irritations and workarounds turn into major bottlenecks and aggravation. This is such a prevalent problem that using those spreadsheets, led us to develop Dryrun.

Spreadsheets are still used for one simple reason: they're highly flexible. But even if you know exactly what you're doing and are experienced in building sophisticated spreadsheets, issues will begin to rear their ugly head. As a friend of mine once complained, spreadsheets quickly "turn into Frankenstein" as more and more data is added and connected. They begin to feel like a house of cards, one mistake and the entire system comes crashing down.

Of course, spreadsheets are still highly useful and valuable in their place, but they are no longer the way manage a business. They're a bit like a favorite bicycle sitting in the garage. It may be comfortable and familiar, but compared to the new car sitting in your driveway, it's just not as effective as transportation for a long road trip.

Spreadsheets also have some major limitations. First, creating one from scratch takes a significant amount of time in structure and data entry. So much so, that I'd hazard a guess that it's unusual for a user to start with a completely blank slate. The most likely first step is exporting data from another system, or customizing a template that doesn't quite fit. That process can work okay the first time but the data is often out of date the minute that it's exported. If the spreadsheet were a single-use tool, running the business this way might be ok, but processes related to financial forecasting need to be maintained as a regular, consistent task.

Moving beyond manual tasks on a spreadsheet takes time and a thorough understanding of the tool. Sophisticated equations and dependencies can of course be layered into the sheet but they are fragile. One minor mistake and the numbers can be completely off. So, double checking every equation and link is essential, but it's also time and attention consuming.

Possibly the greatest hurdle in using spreadsheets is in understanding, explaining and sharing the critical data. It's difficult enough between two financial professionals that are spreadsheet-savvy, but collaboration becomes a monumental task between a financial pro and a business owner with little experience in the system. The problem is even greater when it comes down to business partners. Often neither partner has formal financial training and discussing the data with clarity can be a challenge.

In fact, we hear about this communication barrier every single day from business owners, that often times are reluctant to share their feelings with their financial advisors. "When I look at those spreadsheets I want to die." "It's like ants walking across a page. I have no idea what I'm looking at." "When I see those spreadsheets…beam me up Scotty! Because I'm done!" I could list a hundred of these quotes. So why do businesses continue to struggle with spreadsheets? Why do accounting professionals continue to deliver their services based on them?

The Era of Cloud Software

Well, until fairly recently, there wasn't much of an option. Fortunately, today, a business of virtually any size can benefit from reasonably priced systems that automate an incredible number of labor-intensive tasks, keep data up-to-date and synced across numerous platforms or business units, and deliver forecasts that are easy to understand, update and share. The cost vs. value equation has never been better.

Now that we know how critical cash flow, sales and growth forecasts are for saving businesses from closure through to helping them thrive and grow, here's the good news – it's not very difficult to set up the system and processes you need. It's efficient. It's highly cost-effective and there are professionals that can take nearly all of the tasks off your plate so that you can spend your time doing what you do best: running your business! In later chapters, we'll talk about how business owners can best engage accounting professionals to help them run their business and we'll peel back the curtain on businesses so that accounting professionals can better understand their clients' needs and refine their own services.

So where do you turn for such a system? The answer is...in the clouds! Cloud computing to be exact. Let's first look at how cloud software can revolutionize your business, and then we'll focus on how the systems come together in a cash flow management solution that's efficient, accurate and integrated.

Referred to by several names, cloud computing enable users to access data through an active Internet connection. This means that software that used to be accessed through a single computer console is now accessed through the Internet from any computer. Simply log in to your account on nearly any internet-connected device and you can access your data. This new paradigm means flexibility, efficiency, reliability, security and much more power. (More on that later…)

There are several reasons to why we think you should consider taking the dive into cloud computing for many business related tasks, including cash flow forecasting.

1. Access

Access to data is possibly the greatest advantage over desktop software. With cloud systems, you can access data and information and from nearly anywhere as long as you have an Internet connection, which is nearly ubiquitous these days. You don't even need your own device. You can securely login on any device; complete your tasks and securely logout. Done...from anywhere in the world!

2. Cost

The traditional desktop software model requires that you buy the package with a large, up-front cost. Generally, the software company commits to small bug fixes and modest updates for a short time period, (often a year) followed by an expensive upgrade to keep your software up-to-date and performing reliably. These yearly costs can be significant for multiple 'seats' or 'logins' in a business and somewhat chaotic as a company of users are all attempting to get the latest version of business-imperative software up and running.

By contrast, in the cloud model, each user pays a modest monthly charge and the subscription can be turned on and off as necessary so you're only paying for what you use. There are usually different feature and performance tiers that allow users to move up and down as necessary. Software updates are seamless, and customer support is generally more approach-able and flexible in their responses.

3. Software Updates

Today's companies have massive amounts of data. To main-tain this information, along with reliable and secure backups, requires carefully maintained hardware. Keeping desktop software up-to-date is even more costly and clunky. New releases for desktop tools are infrequent, labor intensive to update and can often render hardware obsolete.

With cloud tools, updates roll out on an ongoing basis and are generally invisible to the user... at least until a great new feature simply appears. The software is up-to-date when you login. Since cloud services only require a browser, the software generally runs well, even on somewhat older browsers and the latest browser is only a short, free download away.

4. Backups

With desktop software, backups fall on your shoulders (or on the shoulders of your in-house IT staff). Often, when things are running fine and business is busy, there can be a tendency to forget about backups. That is, until something goes wrong. A hard drive dies, panic ensues and the victim (you!) frantically tries to recall the last time there was a backup, how to access it, and how to bridge the gap between the last backup and the current date.

Then there's the backup system itself. Is it just another piece of hardware sitting on your desk? If so, do you ever balance your morning coffee on it? Do you have offsite backups? How regularly do you employ them? When you are in control of the backups and it's worked okay, there's a tendency to think that there's very little risk to you. Unfortunately, that's not often the case. Unless you have a well-defined and automated backup system and processes, including offsite storage, you are only one incident away from a disaster.

Cloud software backs up your data automatically and in the background. This technology is a big part of their business and the world's leading cloud tools are hosted on the world's leading servers with top engineers at the helm. Cloud backups are automatic, frequent, reliable and redundant. Is there some risk? Of course. But I suspect that this risk is exponentially smaller than the do-it-yourself model and significantly more cost effective (since it's simply included in the monthly cost) than tasking an internal IT team with buying, upgrading and maintaining a top-notch backup systems.

5. Reliability

Are cloud services reliable? Well, it's true that you need an internet connection to use the tools. In many places around the world, it's now easier to find a web-connection than a water fountain. Personally, the very occasional time my office internet connection has gone down, I simply swapped over to my phone and used the cellular connection to finish whatever I was doing.

Of course, issues with cloud services and data breaches reach the news on a weekly basis. But, to offer a little perspective, downtime of an hour for a massive, online company can become international news but it's actually pretty rare.

It's true, losing an hour of work to cloud services that are un-available can be frustrating, but coming from the perspective of the business that I started in the late 90s, I can tell you that technology issues appear in the blink of an eye. Often, those problems would plague us for days. I remember driving across town and spending hundreds of dollars to try to recover data off a backup drive I had on my desk. Ironically, the backed up data was no longer shared on any of our production comput-ers and it was now irretrievable.

6. Support

Cloud services are often known for their support. For many cloud software services and tools, getting the help you need is as quick as clicking on a chat link from right inside the software. Service is most often included in your subscription and there's generally numerous ways to get in touch.

One of the greatest benefits is that the support team can access your account and backups if needed. When you're on a desktop, the most they can do is talk you through steps to a possible solution, and those steps often come to a grinding halt when a solution doesn't fall under the software's domain. For instance, if you ask about a backup, they will be quick to point out that the backups fall on your shoulders and you need to provision the equipment to do this.

Further, support for desktop tools often expires within a certain period of time. Don't have the latest release? Well, you could be on your own.

7. Collaboration

Whether your work team is all under one roof, or scattered across the globe, cloud services are built for collaboration. Everyone can access data from nearly anywhere and work on files at the same time. For accountants, this is even more essential, since both you and your clients can access key data at anytime from anywhere.

8. Integrations Power!

The cloud brings ground-breaking and business changing power all packed into three letters – API, an "application program interface." Plainly speaking, when cloud software, such as leading cloud accounting tools, offer an API, they are offering a way to connect other cloud apps to their system so that they can all work together.

Modern cloud tools aren't attempting to be "all things to all people" they are specializing in what they do best. Think of it this way: instead of hiring the local repair person for a monumental and complicated job. They may be competent in a wide variety of areas but not an expert in anything particular. Conversely, imagine hiring a team of the world's top engineers, each able to tackle a highly specific and high priority job, and for essentially the same price. Anyone would agree that hiring a team of experts is preferable, as long as they communicate effectively, which is where the API comes in.

With the cloud, not only do you get your team of world-leading tools connected together, you get a package that offers unprecedented power that is tailor-made to your individual business needs – and for a price that is manageable for nearly any business.

Is it Time to Jump to the Cloud?

It's no surprise that cloud technology has an increasing number of advantages over a desktop based licensing system. The cloud environment is still emerging, so best practice is to find libraries of cloud tools to make sure you've found the best options for your business.

The Foundation of Your System, Cloud Accounting

So where do you start? At the core of your 'tech stack' lies a cloud accounting system. Your choice of accounting systems likely has a great deal to do with the surrounding tools that you use in your business.

However, if there is a critical system that you need to run your business efficiently, such as an inventory system, it's likely going to influence other selections, including your accounting system. Start with the most important system first and evaluate the options for integrating other key tools in to the mix.

It's critical to make sure that you are taking the long view within your business. I've seen many businesses severely limit their overall efficiency by focusing their systems on a proprietary piece of software that fails to connect to anything else. The result is data that's trapped. This walled off system in the short term causes headaches but over the long term can cost the business a significant amount of time and money as they move further and further away from high-level efficiencies. Of course, the longer you wait to move to a cloud-based, highly integrated system, the harder the move feels.

A Cloud Software Case Study for business

Today, I run a subscription-based software business; before that, I spent over a decade running a project-based service business. Many of the cash flow, growth and capacity struggles that I experienced then still plague project-based businesses today.

If I had the opportunity to do it again, I know now that a system to help me manage my finances is inexpensive and easy to put in place – I could have engaged an accounting pro for help and really leveraged the equation.

There are hundreds, if not thousands, of cloud apps that can be connected in all sorts of ways, but I'm going to give you one example of how I would set up a system today. These are all apps I am currently using and have experience with, although in possibly a slightly different way that matches my current business.

There are a lot of terrific products that perform a similar function, each with their strengths and weaknesses. It's worth a little time to research each. Talking to a bookkeeper or accountant adept in cloud tools can make your cloud-adoption a much easier and faster process.

Expenses:

My accountant and I currently use a receipt management tool to manage my business expenses. I've connected nearly all of my regular, recurring expenses to the system so that the invoices are automatically sent and archived every month without requiring any additional action. It also lets me login and see nearly any bill that's been charged to my business, clearly organized and quick to access.

For the 'one-off' purchases, I simply forward the emailed receipt to system and use a photo feature to snap a photo of paper receipts and it stores and organizes the information. All of my expenses are tracked with little manual data entry.

When tax time comes around, I still need more than a simple database of expenses to maximize my accountant's time and knowledge. My accountant also needs a record of my income and what's been happening in my bank account to make sure my business finances are clear and correct.

Accounting Platform - The Central Piece:

There are many great cloud-based accounting tools. My own business uses a leading cloud accounting tool recommended and utilized by my accountant. He connected the receipt management tool with a few clicks, so now all of the receipts are automatically entered into my accounting software. I've also connected my business bank accounts and credit card so everything is entered and tracked without me lifting a finger.

Of course, all of this data has to be reconciled to make sure it's all correct. That may be your job, or your bookkeeper's but we're talking minutes every month instead of hours. While we're on the topic, consider setting a goal to hire an accounting professional if you've so far been doing your own books. In the vast majority of cases, an accurate cost analysis will reveal that the value of a cloud-enabled bookkeeper is well worth the cost.

Invoicing:

Next, you need to send out invoices that are clear, professional and that are logged in the accounting system. Well, most cloud accounting tools have you covered there as well. After a quick set up, users can send invoices either directly from their accounting tool or connect and auto-import invoices into the tool. Now they have their revenue ready for an accountant's scrutiny.

Sales Management Software:

Cloud-based sales management software is the perfect antidote for businesses that need to close fewer, but larger sales. The software system is intuitive enough for a business owner to use to keep track of potential deals, notes on client conversations, and next steps to be undertaken, as well as how likely deals are to close, how much they will be worth and when they're expected to close. It's also powerful enough to be used by a sales team.

Cash Flow and Sales Forecasting

In my former business, my biggest challenge was that there was no way, outside of an error-prone spreadsheet (or maybe a white-board) that I could figure out how all these puzzle pieces fit together, so I invented Dryrun, a software application, that allows the user to answer the following questions, along with many more.

Do I have enough money to make payroll on Friday? To make it through the month and quarter? How are sales looking? Am I likely to make a profit this year and grow?

Most importantly, can I see all of these critical items ahead of time so that I can make better decisions, adjust as needed, and grow my business?

A modern, flexible system, such as Dryrun, connects to your cloud accounting tool, imports your data, and sets up a regular, recurring budget forecast to get a sense of your break-even point and forecast into the future. It helps you keep track of all of those invoices you need paid and 'one-off' bills you still need to pay. Yet, you still have complete control to adjust things to make sure it's accurate and real.

The right forecasting tool lets you move things around based on your best guess of when the money will truly come in to your account, and when you intend to actually pay those bills.

The tool also syncs all of those potential sales deals so you can see how your revenue will likely flow in and turn into cash over the upcoming year.

Today, you can make up a team of connected, cloud-based apps that will completely transform your business. You'll see more opportunities, do less administrative work, and save money all in one fell swoop. You can even engage a bookkeeper or accountant to manage the system, take the last bit of work off your hands and serve as an early warning system.

Totally worth it.

15

Engaging Accounting Pros

As I mentioned in the last chapter, engaging an accounting professional to help you manage your forecasts can be a true game changer for nearly any business. Of course, that could be an in-house staff member but often, outsourcing these tasks is a cost-effective and efficient arrangement.

Everyday, my team and I talk with business users all over the world that want to handle everything themselves. Some are quite successful, but many struggle mightily to stay consistent and reap the benefits of ongoing forecasting.

Even if you're an owner that successfully manages your cash flow management and forecasting, I question whether that's the best use of your time. Rarely are business owners and entrepreneurs trained formally in finance; the result is that they are at an immediate disadvantage. Even for those with enough training, ample time, and detailed attention to their books, prioritization is still the issue. Outsourcing financial forecasts is quite straightforward and a natural fit. It's likely that your business is better served when you spend your time on other high priority tasks in your business?.

Now, I'm not suggesting that you simply let an accounting pro disappear with your data and report once a year. That would be a recipe for disaster and has contributed to stagnant growth in many a business over the past generation. You need to have your eye on your data every week, and know where you sit, but many of the laborious tasks can be released to a professional. The major benefit is that you have a professional keeping an eye on things and serving as an early warning system. It's great value for the money spent.

Here's a typical situation that we see nearly everyday:

A business has some sort of in-house bookkeeping software and they do their own bookkeeping but are chronically behind. The only real attention they give to their books is in sending out invoices, although they are often sent much later than intended. Receipts and bills are left in email accounts, paper receipts are stuffed in boxes and every once and awhile they may be entered into their system.

If (or most likely when) they get overloaded, they simple dump the remainder of the receipts on their accountant's desk at the end of the year. Once the books are in their accountant's hands, the real work begins. The accountant spends premium time doing year-end clean up, resulting in an even longer delay, rendering any data historic and nearly useless, while netting a huge year-end tax bill.

Having gone through this mess, many businesses engage an accounting professional to keep things straight, at least on a monthly basis. This is certainly a major step in the right direction. The books are much more up to date and mistakes are at a minimum.

As we've seen in our earlier exploration of cloud tools, many of the data entry tasks can now be automated and highly simplified. So, does that mean you can start managing all of your bookkeeping duties in-house? I'd say no, it's not a great idea.

Bookkeeping is undergoing some significant disruption and major changes are afoot in the industry. Today's cloud-enabled bookkeeper role tends to be quite different from at any point in the past. Bookkeepers set up and manage a business' 'tech stack' - in other words they help select and connect the various cloud tools required to build your system, and onboard your staff to proper usage. They'll also make sure that your data is properly reconciled and up-to-date so that you can login to any system at any time and see recent data.

Finally, and most importantly, bookkeepers and accounting pros can keep your forecasts up-to-date and keep an eye on things, alerting you to possible issues well ahead of time. Think about it - your bookkeeper knows your business intimately. It makes sense to give this person the tools and insight to help steer the business, and then solicit their expert opinion on how to avoid risk and plan for growth.

Using effective and accurate forecasts in your business lessens the number of tasks that you are responsible for while maximizing the impact of the tasks that are left. You'll likely deal with some mission-critical tasks, such as sending out and following up on invoices. You may also manage receipts that aren't automatically imported, but automation will take care of the bulk of your duties in this regard.

Here's an example of a very effective workflow that we often see:

1. Your accounting pro reconciles your bookkeeping weekly to make sure your numbers have been entered correctly. They'll note any questions that they might need you to answer.

2. Your accounting pro refreshes your forecasts and updates the data to reflect reality. In other words, they'll take note of outstanding invoices, bills and other potential issues.

3. They reach out to you with a quick email containing a short to-do list, such as following up on a critical overdue invoice. Ideally, your to-do list is only a couple of items and a few minutes to complete.

4. You reply with your answers and they update the forecast accordingly. You're now up-to-date and can login at any time to see things first-hand and build out some 'what if' scenarios.

5. You, or your sales staff, update and track your sales forecasts to make sure you're on-point.

6. Once a month, your advisor checks in with an overall update and you can discuss other future-focused issues, such as revenue forecasts and growth plans, potential disruptions and other 'what ifs.'

A process such as this keeps you up-to-date on your near-term cash flow by the week. Your to-do list remains short and is managed over the month. Your books are always recently reconciled, presenting the side benefit of always being ready for tax season. You've retained a pro to look over your numbers and created an avenue to have them consistently monitor and report on potential issues so that a brewing crisis can be dealt with while it's still a little problem.

You also have an accounting pro watching your back on a regular basis and offering input on future goals and growth. Instead of paying a big bill right after tax time every year then receiving reports on past performance, you're looking ahead every week. You've just made a necessary reporting task into a consistent, ongoing view into the inner workings and direction of your business. That's putting money to good use by wringing out every bit of value that you can from your own data.

One word of caution. Not all accounting professionals are either equipped or willing to offer ongoing advisory services that will fit your needs. Some firms prefer to focus exclusively on tax returns so they are unlikely to be a good fit for you month to month. Business is much too risky to settle for inadequate systems and service. Make sure every dollar you spend on your accounting services is offering a true benefit every month to your business.

The good news is that there are amazing accounting professionals that are driving the industry forward by offering their clients true value through their advisory services tied with leading edge technology.

I strongly encourage you to evaluate your business needs and ensure that you have the information and service you require for your business. A transition to a highly effective and efficient system is not only essential for managing and growing your business but is also highly cost-effective for the value you receive. In fact, I've even seen costs reduced when businesses move from the annual cleanup and filing to a monthly service that offers so many more benefits.

Finding the right pro to help you is simply a major win for you.

Part 5

For Accounting Professionals

Deliver the Service Your Clients Need

Hello advisory professionals: accountants, bookkeeper, controllers, CFOs, business coaches – the list goes on. If you offer advisory services, this section is for you, but I'll be referring to you (sometimes incorrectly!) as accounting pros. As you've read throughout this book, I've been promoting you to business owners, at every turn, as the key to successful and efficient forecasting.

We see this everyday at Dryrun (dryrun.com) with our accounting pro partners. They are truly changing the game for their clients and building up their own practices in the process. But I also know that we're just scratching the surface. Offering modern, data reconciliation, system management and advisory services is still not the norm, and there are several reasons why that's the case. In this section, I'll provide some insight into the business owner mentality, their needs, and outline the best way to use cash flow forecasting as a core service in your practice.

First, a little background so you can get a sense of where I'm coming from. As I've mentioned throughout the book, I am a co-founder of Dryrun, a cloud-based cash flow forecasting tool. I've shared the struggles I had in my own businesses that led me to create Dryrun and why I'm so passionate about helping business owners tackle their cash flow monster. I simply couldn't find a tool that would deal with cash flow, sales and growth scenarios and let me tackle all of the 'what ifs' I faced every day.

Dryrun takes a truly unique scenario-based approach to forecasting, combining full automation with complete manual control. Short term cash flow forecasts, mid-term sales forecasts and long term growth planning in one, integrated and simple to use app. Ok, that sounds a bit promotional, I know. But let me tell you how we got to this point and made a system, process and tool that helps you offer advisory services that your clients will love.

Initially, I built Dryrun completely for the business owner with zero thought to the accounting world. That's my dirty little secret. But let me share with you why I mistakenly (but fortunately) took this path because it will shed light on some key issues you may face with your clients today.

Going back to my introductory story at the beginning of this book, where I shared the near-death struggles my business faced in 2009 during the recession, there was something I left out. When I was battling to take control of our cash flow, it never even occurred to me that my accountant or bookkeeper may have been able to help.

In my mind, my bookkeeper did data entry and my accountant filed our taxes. Oh yeah, and after our taxes were filed we'd get our 'report card' (financial statements) that told us how good or bad we did. Honestly, those reports meant very little to me. I remember in those meetings, looking over reports, nodding and agreeing with whatever was said but in my mind I bounced between "I know, I was there!" and "I have no idea what you're talking about." That's just the honest truth.

All I wanted to do was to get back to the office and figure out my next move, the past was over and done with. I realize I was being a bit harsh. There was certainly some useful info in those reports but the once a year, already out-of-date data just didn't seem mission critical, and in reality it wasn't. It was useful, but not game changing. I'll admit, the "how much am I paying for this?" question did roll around in my head.

Talking with hundreds of business owners over the years and on a daily basis, I can attest to the fact that many still share this belief. So, when I sold my last business and dove into battling this cash flow issue head-on, it never even occurred to me to ask an accountant any questions. I actually remember thinking that accountants would laugh at a simple-to-use cash flow tool, but I knew that it was the difference between life and death for business owners.

Fast forward to our initial release of a Dryrun prototype. We had our first business-owner customers from different corners of the globe. But a strange thing happened. We kept getting accountants coming out of the woodwork to talk to us. They were really excited about Dryrun. Wait...what!? Then we started getting accounting pros buying subscriptions for Dryrun. We found out that many of our business customers were actually in-house accounting staff. Mmm, I think I really missed the mark on my initial judgment of the accounting industry. If we do this right, they will love us!

Once we released our full commercial version, we were talking to accounting pros on a daily basis. We discovered that their industry was undergoing major disruption. With the rapidly adopted cloud-technology, so many data related tasks were simply taken off their plate. Billable hours were disappearing and businesses were attempting to handle many of the book-keeping tasks in house. (I say attempting because the do-it-yourself method of data handling and reconciliation was often less than successful, but I digress.)

The talk of the industry was in transitioning to offering advisory services. Services that included consultation and set-up of their 'tech stack,' which means advising on, and setting up their system of cloud-connected apps. It includes monitoring the system and reconciling data to ensure it's complete, accurate and up-to-date for use by the business but also ready for tax time.

But something else came up over and over again. Cash flow forecasting was a key service that their clients were dying for, and a perfect advisory service for the new-world accounting pro.

While we were learning more and more about the challenges and opportunities the accounting industry faced, we were discovering that, similar to the do-it-yourself bookkeeping, do-it-yourself cash flow forecasting had a bit of a spotty record among business owners. Even though they knew, or at least suspected, how critical forecasting was for running a successful business, they were dropping the ball for many of the reasons outlined earlier in this book. They were often failing to forecast consistently and diving back into their cash flow only whenever a crisis hit. Not ideal.

While we were talking to accountants on a daily basis about their needs and goals, we began promoting to business owners the benefit of engaging a pro to help them. You can't imagine how many business owners nearly fainted in relief. How many "oh my god, they can do that?!" comments came our way.

Hmm. What's going on here? Accounting pros are driven to offer advisory services, often with cash flow as the cornerstone, and business owners are dying for the help. But it was happening far to infrequently. What gives?

We began to unravel the mystery.

"What we have here is a failure to communicate!" [6]

There seems to be a rather simple, but fundamental problem preventing a perfect advisory relationship. Accounting pros and business owners simply speak two different languages. Now, I know, many accounting pros also own businesses, and many of you are excellent communicators. But there's a fundamental difference between those that have formal financial training and those that don't. The massive difference in financial literacy creates an incredible barrier to communication between the two groups. In fact, your clients likely really struggle with financial concepts.

A recent small business survey, conducted by Intuit, found that despite the fact that 64% of small business owners considered financial management a priority, **83%** of respondents scored at a **basic or failing** level of financial understanding.[7] To be clear, that doesn't mean your clients are not business experts. On the contrary, they are experts in their field and in their own business. But, with little to no formal financial training, there's a good chance your clients struggle more than you believe to understand what you're trying to communicate.

Here at Dryrun, we're really fortunate to bridge the gap between accounting pros and business owners, having in-depth conversations with both groups every day about their greatest challenges. When we talk to business owners we find something really strange. They will often open up to us about their business with absolute brutal honesty right out of the gate. We've even coined a term 'confessional' for these chats. That isn't a tongue-in-cheek term, nor are we making light of their honesty. In fact, many times, these chats can be heartbreaking. "I imported my data, and I'm out of cash next week! What do I do!?"

Entrepreneurs have the weight of the world on their shoulders and are dying for help. We may be cash flow experts, but we're not business advisors. So, we quickly steer the discussion to the topic of their accounting pro. Do they have a trusted advisor that can help them? Unfortunately, all too often they haven't reached out or shared their true feelings with their advisor and rarely intend to. So what gives? Why would they trust us almost immediately but hide critical problems from the advisors that they've trusted with so much of their financial foundation?

Being an entrepreneur for a couple of decades, I'm a long-time member of the community and it didn't take long to discover how this community works. Really, from day one when you take the leap into the deep-end and start a business, you're a part of a tight-knit group of like-minded risk takers. Within a short time of running a business, reality hits and what seemed like a smooth ride with a bump here and there, turns into a daily battle to get over the next ridge.

Of course, finances are likely the greatest stress for business owners, especially new entrepreneurs, but the battles they face come from all sides. Staff problems, delays, cranky customers, dead-beat suppliers. They can barely sit for a minute without another crisis dropping in their lap.

When I run into another entrepreneur, the conversation inevitably turns to the realities of business, the struggles, petty annoyances, all the way through to business disrupting problems. Entrepreneurs can talk for hours, and often do. Too often, in their own business, they have no one to turn to, who can relate to their struggles. Maybe they have a partner they chat with on a daily basis, but a fresh perspective and a different set of ears is always appreciated. Yet, I know the norm is that they stop short of having those brutally honest and to-the-point conversations with their advisors.

So, why is that the case? Their advisors can likely ask the right questions and offer valuable insight. Well, there are a few reasons that I believe lead the way. First, similar to my belief years ago, many business owners simply don't know that their accounting pro can, or will take interest in their challenges, whether they are financially related or not. And, the truth is, some accounting pros do show little interest in helping. But, if you're reading this book, I believe you likely have both the desire and the motivation to help.

Often, the conversations with their accountant to date have been focused on their tax returns, and possibly a brief overview of their financial statements. There's a good chance much of the content covered in the meeting is a bit of a puzzle for the average entrepreneur.

When other business owners, colleagues and friends have the same experiences they just perpetuate the myth amongst the entrepreneur community. I've rarely had a conversation with another business owner where they praise the virtues of their advisor. They may love them, but it just never comes up unless I pursue the point.

Truthfully, business owners often feel intimidated by their advisor and are uncomfortable discussing the finer points of their finances with them, let alone opening up about their future challenges. Even when discussions are on-point, business owners are more likely to clam-up than ask for clarification when the conversation takes a turn into unfamiliar territory. I even recall a customer of ours, receiving cash flow spreadsheets from their advisor and entering all of the data manually into Dryrun, just so she could try to figure out what it was saying! But she refused to tell their advisor she struggled with the data because she didn't want to look stupid.

The fact is that business owners often understand more than they give themselves credit for. They are often well-equipped to put important data into context and take action, but only if they were willing to open up and seek clarification where they struggle with financial concepts.

I've outlined the communication problems in general but let's look at some specific examples of where communication breakdowns routinely occur.

A Partial Picture and Prioritization

Are you hitting on the issues that are top-of-mind for your client? Are you pinpointing problems that are keeping them awake at night? The truth is that you are likely only privy to a fraction of the challenges business faces. You have access to past financial data, but how up-to-date is the data? Do you know where their cash sits today?

Even if their 'books' are virtually up-to-the-minute, when you're not working directly in the business, your view is likely limited. There's surely a tidal wave of issues, plans, opportunities and upcoming challenges that you simply are unaware of. Unfortunately, you may only become aware of the fundamental problems after-the-fact.

Data, insight and observations only have significant value when they're acted upon. For business owners pulled in hundreds of different directions, information-overload, or the feeling of an insurmountable challenge, may push them to virtually ignore the data. As critical as that information may be, it needs to be important in their mind, not yours. They need to have a crystal clear focus on the problem, it can't be mixed into a cloud of issues. That means that you need to understand as much of the overall picture of their business as possible. Today's *and* tomorrow's picture.

After all, your role is no longer about transactional data, rather it's all about teasing out the insights. That means analyzing the data in the context of your client's business.

Quality vs. Quantity

In my experience, business owners want a simple, clear message that hits on the top issue they face – a message that they can use to take action. And they want to take action where it will move their business forward.

Even though you may not have access to the entire picture within a business, you do have access to a lot of data. So, how do you deliver that information so that your client can make best use? Sometimes the tendency is to deliver as much data as possible. That way, your client can pick out the key points and put it to good use. The problem is that it leads to information overload for your client. They are likely unable to pick out the important data point out of the flood of information.

The business owner needs, simple, clear and focused info. Take a look at Fig. 9. What seems more valuable to you, the image of an in-depth and detailed circuit board? Truth be told, the business owner likely prefers the super simplified version that cuts away all of the extraneous details and focuses on the key focal point. They understand that. They can take action on that. That's what they truly value. You understanding what info is most important today. What they can take action on today.

So, how do you determine what information to cut away and how do you deliver just what's critical? It comes down to asking a lot of questions, the right questions and truly listening to the answers. Focusing on the essentials before you outline and deliver the info. In the end, you may be providing all the data BUT you will be able to highlight areas of concern, draw attention to specifics and point out details based on your understanding of the current state of their business.

In other words, instead of simply walking through every point on your forecast or report, hoping they will tease out the important details themselves, draw attention to why a detail or two requires special focus. As an advisor, that's where your true value sits. It's when you further their understanding of their own business, their current situation and empower them to take action. You're acting more as a coach that helps to focus on key areas you observe to be important. If you simply just try to hit every point without educating your clients and putting critical data in context, you will fail to offer true value.

Fig 9. A Complex vs. Simple Circuit Board

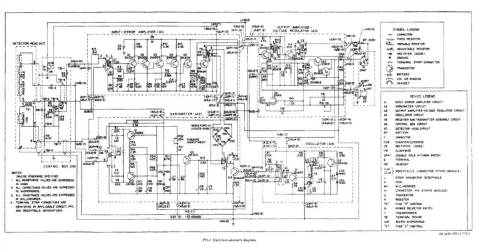

VS.

Electrical Circuit

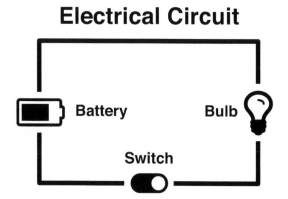

Remember, that one of the most precious commodities a business owner has is time. When they are giving you their time, they need the time to be well spent and fruitful. Questions are your best tool for making the most of your time.

Asking questions will not only help you focus on what really matters right now, but also shows your client you are interested in helping them with the problems that truly plague them. I think sometimes that people believe asking questions will reveal that they're uninformed – that they should already know the answers. That couldn't be further from the truth. Questions show that you understand them and are eager to help them battle their core issues.

In fact, often questions are your key advisory tool. Asking the right questions helps your client identify their problems and as you dig further with follow-up questions. Their understanding will continue to increase.

Business owners often crave the broad strokes and the 'big picture' while accounting pros want to deliver detailed, concrete and perfect answers. The fact is that a forecast will never be perfect and it isn't expected to be. You are there to broaden their view and bring important factors to light.

You're trying to light their path and point them in the right direction, not pick them up and carry them.

Forming the Perfect Match

The first thing to understand is that in a perfect situation, there are definite roles and responsibilities that make an advisor-client relationship result in big rewards and benefits to both sides.

Your client is a wealth of information about their business and the direction they are heading but it's very likely that this information is unorganized, unrecognized and offering little to the business beyond powering the owners intuition. On the flip-side, the accounting professional has formal financial training and expertise that is no less valuable to the business. The key is in understanding that the perfect working relationship requires clear duties, effort and a mutual goal to work.

As we've discussed earlier, there's a good chance that the business owner doesn't even realize that you are able to help them in fundamental ways.

Often, one of the initial, and greatest barriers preventing a working relationship is in the lack of a system and regular processes. I'm sure you've seen this problem with some of your clients. Their records and receipts are scattered throughout their office, car and home. They deliver boxes of paper and digital folders full of all sorts of records. This puzzle needs to be put together before the required tax filing and the problems persist from year to year.

So, when you take a deep dive into understanding your clients business and propose a new way of approaching things, your client is likely to show some serious apprehension. Their first thoughts are how much will it cost and how much time will it take? Both are completely valid concerns. When you can put those worries to rest and outline the game-changing value they receive, your client will experience less friction in taking the next step.

It's critical that you focus on the benefits your services offer and how they can transform their business. The system and processes you're proposing will save them time, deliver their own data, up-to-date and in a format that they'll understand. They'll have an unprecendented view forward, helping them to make informed decisions and take action. You'll be right there, watching their back and ready to discuss plans, issues and alternatives. AND, the price will truly be highly cost-effective considering the value they receive.

Why the Cloud is the Path to Pulling this all Together

We've discussed cloud-computing and some of the advantages of the technology in previous chapters, but let's take a look at how it helps you, the accounting pro, offer highly efficient, high-value services to your clients. It truly is the key to revolutionizing your business as well as your clients.

First of all, let's put the spreadsheet argument to rest for good. We're in a post-spreadsheet world for many key business tasks. There are simply much more powerful, user-friendly and connected tools that render spreadsheets obsolete in this context.

They take you too much time to build, update and manage while your clients cringe at the sight. It can be challenging to read a spreadsheet, let alone tease out the key points in the data. When the information is difficult to read and discuss, it fails to be actionable.

Even cloud-based spreadsheets, that overcome some of the version control and multi-user issues fail to maintain up-to-date versions, where cloud tools sync with a click.

Even worse, one wrong move by your client and a broken equation could render the entire data misleading, even worthless. Tracking down a broken equation is not a good use of anyone's time.

It's simply time to abandon legacy tools and take advantage of automation, artificial intelligence and a superior user experience to take over labor-intensive and time consuming tasks so that you can spend the time analyzing data, collaborating with your clients and offering high-value advisory services.

In fact, today's sophisticated cloud-based tools can save you over 80% of your time, and help you communicate efficiently and effectively with your client, so that you're equipped to offer industry-leading service to your clients.

And what happens when you replace those labor-intensive, data entry and management hours with true analysis and advisory services? You can say goodbye to the billable hour and hello to value pricing. The benefits you deliver offer significant value. A stop watch is no longer required, you can charge a fair rate that reflects the value you are offering to your clients.

Tying Together Technology and Service

Let's take a look at the steps to getting to the perfect match:

1. The Client Discovery Meeting

The first step is a meeting to gain a thorough understanding of your clients business from A to Z. That means plenty of questions, careful listening and note taking. Expect to offer very little advice or commentary in this meeting. You're not just uncovering their current financial situation, rather, what challenges do they face in their business every day? What eats up most of their time? What keeps them awake at night? What systems are really broken and causing them headaches? What's taking up most of their time?

As you ask follow-up questions and dig into their business in detail, what system and processes are causing them the most grief? Costing the most money and wasting the most time?

2. System Selection

We've already explored how cloud-computing systems can revolutionize both your business and that of your clients but now it's time to get our hands dirty and set up some world-class systems and processes.

Now that you know their key challenges, you can research various systems that can serve as the center point for their 'tech stack.' Is their greatest challenge inventory? Project management? Accounts payable and receivable? Human resources and payroll? You may not select the tool for them directly, but you can outline some of the tools you've researched and give them a single piece of homework, evaluating and selecting the best system to meet their needs.

Of course, your recommendation needs to take into account the bigger picture, data sync and future-proofing the system. In other words, it's important to draw attention to tools that will integrate with a leading, cloud-based accounting system. One that not only connects with their mission-critical apps, but also has a varied and robust number of app partners to solve other current problems as well as considering potential future needs.

In order to build a time-saving, data consistent and reliable system, the main tools simply need to be connected. Additionally, as their business evolves and the app ecosystem grows, they're likely to be able to continue to enhance their system with more connected apps.

3. System Set-up

System set-up is certainly a challenge but the more you can take off your clients plate, the better. When they see the time-savings, money-savings and valuable data they can harness in their business, they will be willing to pay a fair price to have the system set up. The more you can take off their hands, the happier they will be.

Now, maybe you don't believe you have a particular strength in setting up these systems, but can offer significant value in the ongoing management, data reconciliation and advisory side of things. Well, you're in luck. There are increasingly more and more independent contractors that have carved out a niche doing exactly what you require. They contribute to system selection, dive in and tackle setup, then hand the reins over to you and your client.

Ongoing Advisory Services

Once the system is up and running, you can transition into regular, consistent services that ensure up-to-date and accurate data, refreshed forecasts, and simple, clear advisory services.

It's consistent, clear forecasting that offers ongoing value. The additional time the highly automated and intuitive systems give you more time to analyze data, point out trends, highlight potential issues, ask questions and offer insight to your clients on a weekly basis.

It's a perfect match.

Business owners desire high value for their money. They can truly harness forward-looking data, delivered in plain language, offering the flexibility required to tackle complex business issues. They also appreciate having their books continually up-to-date so that they are prepared for tax season with little additional stress or the annual scramble to get all of the records together.

Accounting professionals want to be highly valued – appreciated and fairly compensated for the services they provide. I've heard numerous times from accounting pros that their clients are 'cheap.' I can assure you, nothing could be further from the truth. When a business owner sees value and a significant return on their investment, they will spend the money at the drop of a hat. Conversely, when they don't believe they are receiving value for their money, they will refuse to spend a dime. For business owners, it is all about value for money. Offer extreme value and they will happily pay your bill.

19

How to Thrive in the New World

Customer Service vs. Service Packages

As we've explored throughout this book, offering highly effective and valuable services for your clients can, and often will, differ greatly between different clients. Knowing that clients are more than happy to pay top dollar for services with high value, but are loathe to spend a penny on services they view as extraneous, it's critical that you focus on their needs and deliver the perfect-fit service package to each client.

I'm about to make many of you cringe...but hear me out. I strongly discourage productized, service packages. I'm sure you've seen these price lists, maybe you even have a page on your site. It shows a small, medium and large 'package' and the price. I suspect these pricing pages became popular because of the daily calls from business owners that simply ask how much your services cost.

The problem is that if you make the conversation all about price, it'll be all about price. It's much more effective to stand out for your service and the benefits you offer.

I'll let you in on a little secret, business owners really aren't that concerned with price. (Just take a look at their receipts and you'll see all sorts of 'interesting' purchases!) They just don't know how else to compare your services to your competitors and don't necessarily place a high value on the service. They simply ask the only thing that comes to mind. It's your job to educate them on how valuable your service is and how much more you can offer than your competitors.

So, when the question of price comes up, instead of falling into the trap and talking about price first, turn the conversation around and prove to your potential client that you want to offer them service that's perfectly matched, fairly priced and highly valuable for their investment.

Imagine the phone call that comes into your office:

Version 1

"How much do you charge?"

"We have three packages on our website that range from X to Y."

Your potential client jots down the figure, thanks you for your time and phones the next candidate on their list. Not only did you not stand out, you made their decision all about price. It's a dive to the bottom. Let others play that game.

Version 2

"How much do you charge?"

"We only charge for services that are a perfect for your business so that you aren't wasting money on anything that's unnecessary. We offer our services on a monthly basis at minimum so that you're numbers are always up-to-date and include regular updates so that you always know where you stand. We believe in delivering significantly more value and expertise for your dollar. Can I ask you some questions about your business?..."

Once you transition to questions, you'll be able to prove that you care about their business, their experience and offering perfect-match service. Those questions will also help you determine if the lead is a *good fit for you*!

So, I highly recommend outlining your client-focused approach and key benefits on your website to attract customers that are seeking true value and leave simplistic pricing to your competitors as they battle it out in an undercutting price war.

Niche is the New Black

Using the power of cloud software makes it much easier to offer your services remotely to a much broader geographic area. Paired with your growing knowledge in key areas of business, and evaluating your current client list, you can identify your best clients. Those clients that you love to work with and the ones that pay you well for your service.

I highly recommend considering focusing your practice on a niche that you can really dig your teeth into. Building your business on a niche helps you become an expert in the specific challenges that businesses in the sector face. You are more likely to limit the amount of software you need to support as core tools in your business and you will be better able to advise your clients on industry specific needs.

Serving a niche market has other major advantages. You are more likely to gain referrals from existing customers that tend to network within their own communities. It's also much easier to target your marketing and sales efforts on a niche market. You'll likely increase your efficiency and generate more profit in your service offerings through your familiarity with typical client needs and tasks.

Pursuing a high-value niche market can help you leave unprofitable clients behind. Simply put, you can have fewer, more lucrative clients and a higher level of enjoyment during the long hours you put into your business.

Now, it's critical to note that focusing on a niche market only offers these benefits, if it's a large enough market full of businesses that value what you offer and have the money to pay for your services. In other words, high risk start-ups battling to bring back the VHS video store, might not be a niche to pursue.

Cash Flow Forecasting Can Lead the Way

Circling back to the topic of this book, the number one killer of businesses and the challenge holding so many businesses back from success and growth, cash flow management, is a true opportunity for you to offer significant value to your clients. Cash flow management builds on the other services you offer month to month, such as data reconciliation, but defines itself through it's high value to your clients. Taking cash flow data and offering an early warning system, oversight and advisory services can power the value you offer to your clients, becoming a central service for your practice.

Your total package of services may include prescribing and setting up cloud systems, reconciliation, prep for taxes, special advisory services and even tax filing. But cash flow forecasting can serve as the week-to-week, month-to-month service that puts their data to use in a form that is highly valuable and informative. It lowers their risk, helps them deal with disruption and plan for sustainable growth. A properly selected system can even give your clients a tool for managing their revenue projections in a broader forecast, while letting you keep an eye on the bigger picture.

So what's preventing you from taking the leap and transforming your own business alongside that of your clients? It often goes back to the start of this chapter. A failure to communicate.

Talking with Your Clients

I've left this topic for the end but it's critically important. In fact, we find that one of the greatest barriers when accounting professionals want to offer advisory services, especially with a focus on cash flow forecasting, is in the delivery of the service to their clients. In other words, we find accounting pros and business owners speaking two different languages.

I can speak for the business owner/entrepreneur since that's my background. We've got way too much on our plate. We're pulled in a hundred different directions daily and we're putting out fires constantly. We know that cash flow is critical, in fact we know cash flow intimately...if intuitively. We're the ones that are putting off our own paycheck or putting in our own cash to keep the business afloat. Trust me, we know what cash flow is. Far from being illiterate or tuned out, we're simply prioritizing the best that we can.

We regularly have sleepless nights, dreading either a crisis or the excitement of triumph. We may not be financial experts but we are experts in our own business and operations, whether we recognize that fact or not.

However, we often feel like things are out of our control. We have a sense that working harder will solve all the problems we face. We don't spend enough time and attention dealing with our cash flow because we're not sure how to do it, we're not confident that a process will really help, and sometimes, we just 'don't want to face it.' We want a solution that makes our life easier, not more complicated.

We're not overly cost conscious, but are **highly value conscious**. In other words, if we don't see the value, we won't spend a dime, but if the value is there, cost is no object (within the realities of business.)

So, where do things go wrong? First, it's in understanding the clients' true needs. Not what you perceive from the outside but what you can offer that will help them take action. Second, it's in communication. They want simple, clear, to-the-point and highly focused data. Third, make it all about them and fitting their business, their needs and their culture. It's all about them, not about fitting them into your 'box.'

How You Can Offer Value

1. Truly understanding your clients needs

Offering the right solution rests on you understanding what your client truly needs and delivering services that solve their core problems. That question can't be answered by looking at their past records. Those records only give a fraction of the picture.

Truly understanding their business requires a series of deep-dive conversations with your client. That engagement is only effective if you are asking the right questions and narrowing in on their true issues. Develop empathy for their mindset and barriers, and then strive to understand their challenges intimately so that you can use your expertise to properly advise them.

Your number one tool for uncovering those needs is rather simple. It's a focus on asking questions rather than prescribing solutions. That comes later. You are likely, to run into some struggles as you ask your questions. You are likely to uncover areas of misunderstanding and limited knowledge within your client. Don't skip over those areas, focus on them. Here's where education helps to move things forward.

So, where do you start? Well, that will depend on you gauging each client's level of financial literacy and identifying blind spots. There are several resources that I've included in the appendix which can serve to help both educate and prompt conversation.

Resource Overview

First, a Cash Flow Scorecard. (Appendix A.) It consists of ten, plain-language questions, each ranked from one to five. The questions help your client to identify and discuss the greatest cash flow challenges that affect their business. It also offers a final tally that can be an indication of the risk level a business faces.

There is a printable flowchart of a basic business schematic that can help you discuss common cash flow pinch points. Visualizing the flow of documents and money can help focus the conversation on high areas of concern. (Appendix F.)

You will find two cash flow diagrams that deal with the unpredictable nature and timing problems that frequently plague cash flow. (Chapter 3.) The "iceberg" graphics can help demonstrate the issues that cause businesses to deal with late payments and frequent shortfalls. It can also help illustrate how important it is to manage cash flow in a consistent and sophisticated system, rather than relying on memory to keep track of the everything.

There is a basic diagram in Chapter 1 that simplifies revenue, profit and cash flow and in Chapter 5 you will find, two diagrams that explore risk reduction versus opportunity that forecasting offers.

In Chapter 6, there's an illustration that breaks out the five aspects of forecasting, from crisis and risk reduction (the areas where accounting pros often focus) through to revenue goals and growth planning where your client plays. These areas offer additional opportunities to offer high value advisory services.

Appendix B & C are resources to help address late payment issues that so many businesses suffer from on a daily basis.

I've even included a basic list of questions and topic areas in Appendix D. to help you begin your conversations and a forecasting frequency matrix in Appendix E.

I've seen how effective using simple, clear diagrams and resources can be for prompting conversations and understanding your client's barriers. That understanding will lead you to prescribing the right solution for each client – the solution that they truly value.

These resources are available in downloadable, shareable and printable formats at **pandemiccashflow.com.**

2. You fit their box, they don't fit yours

If you've done step one correctly, with an open mind and a focus on your customer's success, you will find that you need to adapt to clients to some degree, rather than demanding that they adapt to you and your practice. In other words, offering true value may mean adjusting the delivery of your services to meet their needs, even if it represents a break from your typical offering, especially if you are still in the 'package' mindset.

Each of your clients are likely to face a unique set of circumstances and their needs can vary significantly. The size of the business, annual sales, risk level and even the ease of working with the business owner can greatly affect the relationship and service delivery. The larger the business and the more complex their need, the more likely they'll require highly customized services. However, the larger the business and the more complex their problems, the more potential value you can offer.

More value means more money, for both of you. So, trying to pigeonhole every business into a basic package is likely to push your potentially most valuable and profitable clients to a competitor that offers customized, perfect-fit services at a premium rate.

The key to building a successful advisory service business is to offer significant value and charge based on that value, not on a ticking clock.

Remember, if you make the conversation about price rather than the value, you will be judged on price rather than value. That approach inevitably leads to a race to the bottom where you will battle it out with more and more competitors offering lower and lower prices.

Meanwhile, the most valuable clients are being educated and better served by industry leading advisors charging fair, yet premium rates.

3. Providing Actionable Data

I've also seen both sides of this coin repeatedly. Business owners are highly goal-oriented. They want to take action and solve problems. That means that they want clear, actionable data that's laser focused.

Business owners need quality data that they can act upon. Quality isn't necessarily about accuracy, in fact, forecasts will never be perfect and the farther out they reach, the higher variance you'll see between forecast and reality. That does not mean that the data isn't valuable and critical. Quality to a business owner means that it's high priority, topical, focused and clear.

They need clear direction. Imagine this conversation as part of a weekly check-in: "Please look into Invoice #4587, it's eleven days overdue and a big one. You need that cash coming in to cover your materials for your next job. Follow up on that today!" That's simple, clear, high priority and actionable.

Imagine delivering this instead: "Here's your P&L, income statement and cash flow statements. Talk to you next quarter."

I know that these comments are highly simplified and I'm not saying that there's no value to financial reports but your top priority is to offer frequent, topical and on-point value that helps them prioritize and take action. Your goal is to offer what your client truly needs.

Cut through the muck and help identify things that will move the needle in their business.

Summing it Up

I can still picture my cash flow spreadsheets from my creative agency. They provided insight that not only helped save our business, but also helped us grow. Fast forward over a decade later and I'm even more passionate about helping business owners manage their cash flow to success. I realized over a decade ago that the systems and processes available to manage the financial foundation of business were simply not there.

Even back then, a Google search would bring up hundreds of articles proclaiming cash flow as the number one culprit in business deaths, yet the solution they shared was nearly always simply, 'use a spreadsheet.' That's it. No real insight into the problem. No help in diagnosing the underlying causes. No process or system that I could follow. Just simply a subtext that said, "you're on your own kid." That's not the news you want when you're in a panic and it feels like the walls are closing in.

It was sometime around 2012 that I started holding coffee meetings, sitting down with dozens of business owners over several months. I'd ask them about their operations and challenges. Did they struggle with cash flow? How did they deal with the issue? I heard over and over again, that "hell-yeah it's an issue!" But they'd either use a spreadsheet, and proclaim their hatred for the tool, or even worse, they didn't track anything at all and simply hoped for the best. I began to understand that my own systems and processes, still in their infancy, we're miles ahead of the norm. That's when the idea to tackle the problem of cash flow truly took hold.

It was less of identifying a 'market opportunity' and more of a 'what the hell!?' sort of approach. Why wasn't anyone trying to tackle this problem? THE problem! So, maybe a little naive, I, Blaine Bertsch, having recently sold a business and really, with no plans for what to do next, decided that I could make this problem my own. I could make a difference.

After mountains of research and work, an ultra-basic prototype, and an endless line of discussions with early customers, my Co-Founder and I launched Dryrun in 2016. (dryrun.com)

Dryrun is really the culmination of over a decade in the trenches of business. Hundreds of discussions with business owners and accounting professionals. Dryrun is a unique product among the industry. It was built from the business owner perspective to deal with the toughest cash flow cases.

Dryrun is scenario-based offering nearly unlimited control to test out 'what ifs.' Dryrun's fully automated in it's data handling, integrates with the some of the world's leading cloud accounting and sale tools, yet maintains complete flexibility and manual control to model out truly complex business problems.

It simplifies the complex and is happy helping you with this week's cash flow and this year's revenue goals, all the way through to your multi-year plans and 'what if' scenarios.

Coming from its roots as a business tool that's highly operational and effective in the trenches has made Dryrun the perfect tool for the accounting professional. It will save them over 80% of their time when compared to using spreadsheets, while delivering forecasts in a system and process that their clients will love.

Our team at Dryrun is truly dedicated to doing our part in crushing the Cash Flow Pandemic.

Thanks so much for reading this book. I would love to hear from you! Please reach out and connect with me at blaine@dryrun.com.

Discover how Dryrun can help take control of your cash flow at dryrun.com.

Endnotes:

1. "Half of All Small Businesses Fail by Year 5 – Here's Why (Infographic)" June 27, 2017 by Shubhomita Bose. https://smallbiztrends.com/2017/06/why-do-small-businesses-fail.html

2. "5 Ways to Tackle the Problem That Kills One of Every Four Small Businesses" May 19, 2015, by Elaine Pofldt. http://time.com/money/3888448/cash-flow-small-business-startups

3. "Cash Flow: The Reason 82% of Small Businesses Fail" Mar 8, 2018, by Michael Flint. https://www.preferredcfo.com/cash-flow-reason-small-businesses-fail

4. My buddy, Mark.

5. "Evidence-based Impacts of Slow Payment Practices in Alberta's Construction Industry: Research Report Compiled for the Alberta Trade Contractors Coalition" Spring, 2015, by Megan Kinal, M.Sc. http://mca-ab.com/wp-content/uploads/2016/05/150901_ATCC_PPL-Survey_fnl-1.pdf

6. Quote from 1967 film Cool Hand Luke, spoken in the movie first by Strother Martin and, later, paraphrased by Paul Newman.

7. "Bridging the Gap – How Boosting Financial Literacy Leads To Small Business Success" by Intuit. http://intuitglobal.intuit.com/delivery/cms/prod/sites/default/intuit.ca/downloads/quickbooks/bridging_the_gap.pdf

Appendix

Appendix A: Cash Flow Check Up & Building a Scorecard

Factors that affect cash flow vary from business to business, both in the level of risk, as well as which factors pose the greatest challenge.

You likely know what your core issue in your cash flow is right now, but bear with me and we may identify some factors affecting your cash flow you may not have considered or we may prioritize factors in a different manner.

Before we jump into your cash flow check up, let's set a baseline with a number of commandments that are required to properly implement and manage your scorecard

1. What gets measured gets done.

You must be convinced that the act of reviewing numbers every week with your leadership team increases awareness, peer pressure, and results. When someone reports on their number it drives action and smokes out inaction. You do not want to find out that you have been riding on 12 days of cash reserves at the end of the calendar year.

2. Keep it simple.

Boil your business down to a handful of numbers. Everyone on the leadership team must have a number, metric, KPI they own. Remember, there is no correlation between profit and promises. The numbers you will report on will help build clarity and will ultimately reflect on your cash flow.

3. Managing metrics saves time and puts your finger on the pulse of your business.

The Scorecard becomes a time-management tool---Building the first iteration should take 30-45 minutes. Sit down with the leadership team and determine the indicators that provide the baseline for your organization. Take 15 minutes per week with your leadership team reporting on the numbers.

4. The Scorecard predicts profitability.

A Scorecard paints a vivid picture of your current reality and foretells your financial future. Inspect what you expect.

5. "Trust but verify."

Healthy accountability is still required, even in a 'high trust' business culture.

6. Inspect what you expect.

Inspecting numbers and requiring accountability doesn't say, "I don't trust you." Trust, commitment and measurement are the reasons that most healthy business cultures are successful, not vice versa.

7. The Scorecard requires discipline and consistency.

This is about execution and measurement, which will allow your organization to evolve over time.

8. One person must own the Scorecard.

One member of the leadership team must ensure that all numbers are filled in each week and 100% accurate. When there are errors and omissions, you lose trust and the process of running your business becomes a hallucinatory event.

Belief

If you don't believe at your core in the above eight truths, your Scorecard will never fully work for you.

Now, let's go through the Cash Flow Check Up for your business, so you can identify the right aspects to include in your scorecard.

1. How do you get paid?

1 ☐   2 ☐   3 ☐   4 ☐   5 ☐

Cash Purchases   Invoices, Net 60+

2. How big are your individual sales?

1 ☐   2 ☐   3 ☐   4 ☐   5 ☐

Lots of customers, small purchases   Fewer clients, larger sums

3. How often do you get paid late?

1 ☐   2 ☐   3 ☐   4 ☐   5 ☐

Rarely   Often overdue by 60+ days

4. How large is your monthly budget?

1 ☐   2 ☐   3 ☐   4 ☐   5 ☐

Small and easily managed   Large and often stressful to cover

5. How do you pay your largest expenses?

1 ☐   2 ☐   3 ☐   4 ☐   5 ☐

Small cash payments   Large bills, due upon receipt

6. How often do you pay your bills past their due date?

1 ☐   2 ☐   3 ☐   4 ☐   5 ☐

Rarely   Frequently have overdue bills on my desk

7. How fast are you growing?

1 ☐   2 ☐   3 ☐   4 ☐   5 ☐

Growth is nearly static   Fast, aggressive and expensive

8. How do you fund expansion?

1 ☐   2 ☐   3 ☐   4 ☐   5 ☐

With a portion of cash reserves   Through loans

9. How big are your savings?

1 ☐   2 ☐   3 ☐   4 ☐   5 ☐

Cover 3+ months of expenses   In debt, drawing on loans/credit

10. Have you ever missed paying yourself?

1 ☐   2 ☐   3 ☐   4 ☐   5 ☐

Never   It happens regularly

How did you score?

Total your score, multiply x 2 and circle items that
scored **4** or **5**. The 4 and 5 scores represent **high risk**
areas to closely monitor.

20 - 46

Your cash flow risk is low which can lead to inattention
and unexpected issues. Establish monthly tracking at
a minimum.

47 - 73

You have moderate cash flow risk with some high-risk
areas that can lead to shortfalls, so monitor regularly and
consider professional help to maintain.

74-100

Your cash flow risk is HIGH. Weekly monitoring is essential
to avoid shortfalls. Engaging a professional to help track
your cash flow is recommended.

My score: _____

Weekly Scorecard, Courtesy of Scott Rusnak

Start by building the first iteration of your Scorecard, by sitting down with the leadership team to determine the indicators that provide the baseline for your organization.

When you have the basics of the initial scorecard, be sure to schedule 15 minutes per week so that each member can report and comment on the numbers they are responsible for.

- One person is accountable for each number

- Report on 5 to 15 numbers

- You've established a goal for each measurable

- If the goal is not hit for the week, identify, discuss and solve during your leadership team meeting

To learn more about establishing EOS and a Scorecard in your business please refer to www.scottrusnak.com

WEEKLY SCORECARD

Who	Category	Goal	Week Beginning							
			21-Jan	4-Feb	11-Feb	18-Feb	25-Feb	4-Mar	11-Mar	18-Mar
Ryan	AP	<30k								
	AR	>50K								
Melissa	Payroll	28k								
	Cash Reserves	>180K								
Jason	Weekly Proposals	8								
	Weekly Client Meetings	4								
	Weekly Clients Closed	2								
Ally	Client Onboarding Sessions	2								
	Client Training Sessions	3								
	Satisfaction Survey Rating	8.5+								

Appendix B. Tactics for Getting Paid Faster

Negotiating Terms

1. Negotiate your first payment up front

Getting some money up front means instant cash flow and ensures that your customers are serious about paying on time. The amount of the initial payment will likely differ from project to project and with each client so discuss early.

2. Progress Payments

One of the worst things you can do for your cash flow (and risk level) is wait until final delivery for full payment. Break up the payments into numerous steps. The number is based on the circumstances. As a rule of thumb, the more payments the better.

3. Request a smaller final payment

Often projects can be delayed when they're nearly complete for any number of reasons and final sign-off can be difficult to obtain. Request a larger payment up front and a smaller payment for final delivery.

ie. For a 5 payment job, Split up as 30% up front, 20%, 20%, 20% and final as 10%.

4. Negotiate the definition of deliverables

Rather than detailing specific deliverables such as '100% completion of wireframes', try to negotiate delivery based on '90% completion of wireframe stage.'

This helps to keep things moving when some minor issue delays completion which can benefit both sides as clients rarely want to slow timelines down either.

Negotiate to invoice progress payments upon delivery rather than upon approval. Waiting for 'sign-off' before you can invoice can cause serious delays.

5. Detail timelines for approvals

Delivering quickly won't matter much if the client takes too long to give you official approval. Detail in the contract a reasonable but short turnaround on approvals and document what is required for official sign-off.

6. Delinquent payments

Having progress payments gives you leverage if payments dry up and you need to stop work. It means that you have some money in hand for work already complete and the client is out-of-pocket, motivating them to keep paying you.

However, pausing projects while you await payment is an extreme measure and, in many cases, can seriously harm your relationship with your client.

Invoicing

7. Invoice as soon as possible!

This seems obvious but often 'work' gets in the way. Make sure you are delivering the promised goods or services as soon as they are ready, requesting approval and invoicing immediately.

8. Send electronic invoices

If you're not already doing so, send invoices via email or invoice online so that it gets there quick and it's easy to confirm it's been received.

9. The devil is in the details

Make sure that your invoices are detailed, correct and contain all necessary information. If you are missing critical info, payment delays are bound to happen.

10. Due Date

A clear due date is a critical element on your invoice. "Net 30" does not have the same urgency as "Due: August 9, 2015."

Due upon receipt might sound good to you but to your client, it really says "due whenever you get around to it." Reminders and collection calls are much easier when there is a clearly stated due date on the invoice.

11. Send to the right person

Invoices routinely sit in an inbox or on a desk rather than making their way to the person responsible for paying them. Ask your contact who you should send the invoice to and ask them if they like to be copied on the communication (cc'd).

This makes it easy for them to give you access to the person responsible for paying you while knowing that they will be in the loop.

12. Approval

Make sure that the work has been approved and you've received formal sign-off before invoicing your customer.

Verbal approvals are a minefield. Make sure that you've received official, written sign-off, even if it's just a simple, clear email, before you send out an invoice. It avoids potential confusion and embarrassment.

13. Follow up

Follow up with your billing contact if you fail to receive confirmation that the invoice arrived.

If an invoice's payment has not been received on the due date follow up immediately to show your customer that you take payment seriously. It also might alert your customer if something is awry with the payment. Just be sure that you are very friendly and professional when you call.

If the invoice is indeed outstanding, regular follow-up is essential, at minimum every ten days. If you are mid-project, that means you can stop spending time on it and divert resources to other areas.

14. Tracking your receivables

Carefully track your invoices and receivables in order to deal with issues and keep the cash flowing. Make sure you have systems in place that help you keep track of your receivables and also maintain up-to-date cash flow projections to warn you of impending issues and potential shortfalls well ahead of time.

The more lead-time you have of a pending shortfall, the more options you have.

Electronic Payment Options

Accepting electronic forms of payment can speed payments up dramatically. Checks are about the slowest form of payment and the type that leads to the most fraud.

15. Request direct deposit from your customer

With larger customers, direct deposit is often an alternative. Generally, these payments are scheduled ahead of time to deposit directly into our bank account on the due date.

16. Accept credit card payments

Accepting credit cards is also much easier than in the past. Multiple services will deal with credit card payments without difficult and expensive set up.

17. Accept alternative electronic payments

Numerous online payment systems, such as electronic money transfers between bank accounts and services like PayPal offer alternatives to the paper check that are fast and more secure.

Your Customer Relationship

A trusted client can make the process of negotiating fair and reasonable terms, acquiring timely approvals and ensuring quick payment an enjoyable one.

18. Build trust with your clients

No matter what size of organization you are dealing with earning trust from your customers is essential. They often have much more wiggle room and pull than you believe.

19. Request flexibility in payments

Clients that trust you and have a long, fruitful history with you are going to be much more likely to go the extra mile to help you out in a crisis. This could include altering timelines to allow you to deliver other work ahead of theirs, or requesting quicker payments tied to a small incentive, such as a discount.

Of course, try to avoid these circumstances and only use rarely as a last resort.

20. Keep your bank on your side

Similarly, when you've had a long and stable relationship with your bank they may be more likely to help when you are dealing with an emergency.

Chronic Payment Issues

21. Charge late fees

For customers that are chronically late in paying their invoices adding a late fee to your invoice can help add urgency to the deadlines. Ensure that you have clearly stated your intention and the fee amount within the contract and on each invoice.

Charging late fees has the potential to harm your relationship with your customer so it's important for you to decide whether the potential risk is worth the reward.

22. Offer Incentives.

Offering an incentive can work to speed up payment. Similar to charging late fees, I generally avoid offering incentives for quick payments unless it fits the business needs.

Incentives are used to speed up payments faster than normal, not for paying on time. For instance, you may offer 2% off payments that arrive within 15 days, rather than the actual deadline of 30 days.

Appendix C: Payment Checklist

Setting Terms in Your Contracts

☐ Negotiated first payment up front

☐ Built progress payments into the contract

☐ Requested a smaller final payment

☐ Negotiated the definition of deliverables

☐ Documented the timelines for approvals

Invoicing Process

☐ Approval has been received

☐ Invoiced sent as soon as possible

☐ Sent electronic invoice

☐ Requested direct deposit

☐ Offered electronic payment

☐ Invoice contained all necessary details

☐ Clearly documented due date on the invoice

☐ Invoice sent directly to the proper person

☐ Invoice due date is carefully tracked

Handling Late Payments

☐ Have followed up on late payments

☐ Offered incentive for quick payment

☐ Have charged fees to chronic late payers

Appendix D: Discussion Points for Business-Advisory Meetings

Topics:

- Objectives, timelines and deliverables across business units

- Discussion of cash flow in its various aspects

- Education around cash flow literacy

- Disruptive elements that might affect cash flow this week, month, quarter and year

- Interim milestones and deadlines that could affect cash flow

- Where projects, deadlines and payments are at

- Specific targets could be streamlined

- Deadlines that might have an impact

- Accounting for your business' overall circumstances and priorities

Appendix E: Forecasting Frequency

Forecasting Outcomes	Timelines	Recommended Frequency
Crisis Management	Near and Mid Term	Weekly/Monthly
Risk Reduction	Near, Mid and Long Term	Monthly, Quarterly
Revenue Goals	Near and Mid Term	Weekly, Semi-Monthly
Growth Planning	Mid and Long Term	As required, Quarterly
Disruption Preparation	Near and Mid Term	As required, Monthly

Business Cash Flow

Vendors and Suppliers

Customers

Marketing

Quote → Proposal → Contract → Invoice → Payment → Receipt

Contract → PO → Bill → Expense

Employees

Payroll → Payment → Pay stub

Bank → Tax

Made in the USA
Columbia, SC
23 December 2019